Gratitude to God When Family Rips Your Heart into a Million Little Pieces

Evangeline N. Asafor, Ph.D.

© 2020 by Evangeline N. Asafor. All rights reserved. IEM PRESS is honored to present this title with the author. The views expressed or implied in this work are those of the author. No part of this publication may be reproduced, stored in a retrieval system, or transmitted in any way by any means—electronic, mechanical, photocopy, recording, or otherwise—without the prior permission of the copyright holder, except as provided by USA copyright law. Unless otherwise noted, all Scriptures are taken from the Holy Bible, New International Version®, NIV®. Copyright © 1973, 1978, 1984, 2011 by Biblica, Inc.™ Used by permission of Zondervan. All rights reserved worldwide. www.zondervan.com

ISBN 10: 1-947662-71-6
ISBN 13: 978-1-947662-71-1

Library of Congress Catalog Card Number: 2020905372

DEDICATION

This is for all the modern-day Josephs, Jephthahs, Abels, Hoseas, Hagers, Ishmaels, Tamars, and anyone who has ever been betrayed by family.

TABLE OF CONTENTS

Acknowledgments 6
Foreword 7
Chapter 1: What is Family? 13
Chapter 2: What is Family Loyalty? 16
Chapter 3: What is Family Betrayal? 19
Chapter 4: Cain and Abel: The First Family Betrayal 23
Chapter 5: The Betrayal of Joseph by His Brothers 26
Chapter 6: The Betrayal of Esau by His Brother Jacob and His Mother Rebecca 32
Chapter 7: Invasion of Privacy: A Shameful Secret Behind Family Betrayals 38
Chapter 8: Lack of Prayers: A Shameful Secret Behind Family Betrayals 44
Chapter 9: Family Jealousy: A Shameful Secret Behind Family Betrayals 48
Chapter 10: The Betrayal of Rachel by Her Father and Her Sister Leah 52
Chapter 11: Family Culture: A Shameful Secret Behind Family Betrayals 56
Chapter 12: The Betrayal of Jephthah by His Brothers 59
Chapter 13: The Betrayal of Hagar and Ishmael 63
Chapter 14: The Betrayal of Hosea by Gomer 66
Chapter 15: Adultery: A Shameful Secret Behind Family Betrayals 70
Chapter 16: The Betrayal of Tamar by Her Half-Brother Amnon 74

Chapter 17: Incest: A Shameful Secret Behind
 Family Betrayals 78
Chapter 18: Adoption: A Secret Behind Family Betrayals 83
Chapter 19: When Your Child Rips Your Heart into a
 Million Little Pieces 87
Chapter 20: When Your Parent Rips Your Heart into a
 Million Little Pieces 90
Chapter 21: When Your Spouse Rips Your Heart into a
 Million Little Pieces 93
Chapter 22: When a Sibling Rips Your Heart into a
 Million Little Pieces 97
Chapter 23: When Relatives Rip Your Heart into a
 Million Little Pieces 100
Chapter 24: Communication Technology: A Medium of
 Family Betrayals 103
Chapter 25: Emotional and Divine Intelligence
 When Dealing with the "Cains" in Your Family 107
Chapter 26: Mental Illness: A Secret Behind Family Betrayals ... 111
Chapter 27: Ignorance: A Shameful Secret Behind
 Family Betrayals 115
Chapter 28: Substance Abuse and Addiction: Secrets
 Behind Family Betrayals 119
Chapter 29: Emotional Stages of Grief After Family Betrayal 126
Chapter 30: Jesus' Take on Forgiveness 133
Chapter 31: In Everything, Give Thanks to God 137
Conclusion: Knowledge, Wisdom, and
 Understanding for the Family 143
Special Acknowledgment 149

ACKNOWLEDGMENTS

To God, my Creator: ABBA Father, I trust in you with all my heart. I refuse to put my confidence in my own understanding. Family has ripped my heart into a million little pieces, and I trust you to ease my pain. In all my ways I acknowledge you. Please continue to heal me and direct my path in Jesus' name, amen.

To my Papa and Mama: You both, in different ways, taught us your children that *sticks in a bundle are unbreakable*, therefore, we should always stick together as a family no matter what! Thanks for being the best parents God ever created.

To my children: My fearfully and wonderfully made offspring: Angela (my Angel), Tiffany (my Treasure), Bryan (my Blessing) and Ryan (my Riches). May Jehovah God continue to bless, protect, and guide you throughout the fulfillment of your destinies in Jesus' name. Amen. Thanks for giving me immense joy.

To my family and friends: Thanks for your unconditional love and support. Let gratitude be your companion wherever you go, and you are sure to enjoy the ride while reaping life-sustaining benefits in Jesus' name. Amen!

FOREWORD

This book When Family Rips Your Heart into a Million Little Pieces titled is the fifth book in the Gratitude series from the emerging stable of this dynamic author. It is important to understand that the concept of family is God's original idea to reclaim the earth after the fall of man. We could recall that God started the redemptive process by selecting Abraham who became the progenitor of the Jewish family through which Christ, the Redeemer, came. For this, I bow my knees unto the Father of our Lord Jesus Christ, of whom the whole family in heaven and earth is named (Ephesians 3:14-15).

Biblically, a family could be physical, and it could also be spiritual. For instance, we have the natural Israel (Jewish) family comprising the descendants of Jacob and we also have the spiritual Israel (Jewish) family comprising all the redeemed people from all nations of the world. For he is not a Jew who is one outwardly; neither is circumcision that which is outward in the flesh. But he is a Jew who is one inwardly; and circumcision is that which is of the heart, by the Spirit, not by the letter; and his praise is not from men but from God (Romans 2:28-29).

The two broad categories of a natural family are nuclear families and extended families. The nuclear family consists of a man, woman, and one or more of their biological or adopted children. The extended family establishes ties across generations; it includes at least three generations comprising grandparents, married offspring, and grandchildren, as well as aunts, uncles, and cousins. The functions of a family include the addition of new members, physical care of members, socialization of children, social control of members, disciplining or teaching children right from wrong, affective nurturance (maintaining morale of members), and producing and consuming goods and services. God sets the solitary in families; He brings out those which are bound with chains, but the rebellious dwell in a dry land (Psalm 68:5). Conversely, the spiritual family includes members of a person's natural nuclear and extended families. It also includes other Christians across the globe that such a person must relate with from time to time, whether as members of the same church fellowship, or other Christian groups or societies.

The primary function of the family is to ensure the continuation of society, both biologically through procreation, and socially through socialization. Family is important because it provides love, support, and a framework of values to members. Family members are expected to help and care for each other, as well as share life's joys and sorrows, thereby providing a platform for personal growth. A good family life occurs when members of a family enjoy each other's company and spend a lot of time doing things together. Family members are thus expected to love and respect each other, or at least tolerate each other, and grow to love and care for each other as they interact. Family members are close-knit and feel they can depend on one another because of the love or common interests that bind them. However, when the family life is characterized by stress and conflict, the health of family members tends to be affected negatively. Family values are important because they are the glue that holds a family together. Accordingly, fidelity, loyalty, duty, respect, and perseverance contribute to a sense of safety and comfort among family members.

It is quite important to realize that family members can provide a person love, care, and support but they can also betray the person whether consciously or unconsciously, and such broken bonds of trust are usually more hurtful than those that come from non-family members. Betrayal is when people you love and trust lie to you, cheat on you, abuse you, or hurt you. It is probably the most devastating loss a person can experience because it makes the person lose trust in the betrayer. It is, however, important to note that betrayal is a natural phenomenon that occurs as a result of the limitation imposed on us by our human nature. Betrayal is also in tandem with the dictum "To err is human, to forgive is divine." Furthermore, the Bible maintained that family betrayal will be rampant in this dispensation. Brother will deliver brother over to death, and the father his child, and children will rise against parents and have them put to death (Mathew 10:21). Therefore, it is advisable that every member in any kind of family should be best prepared for the worst to happen so that when the worst (betrayal) happens, the betrayed family member does not bolt into a shock.

Betrayal includes harmful disclosures of confidential information, disloyalty, infidelity, and dishonesty. It can be traumatic and cause considerable distress because it catches us totally off-guard and it threatens our sense of security. Betrayal also shakes a person to the core because it ruptures the person's ability to trust. The effects of betrayal include shock, loss and grief, morbid pre-occupation, damaged self-esteem, and anger.

It is, however, crucial that a betrayed person should know how to handle the betrayal to mitigate its adverse effects and guarantee a healthy disposition. You cannot change what has happened to you or make the pain go away so easily. Hence, you need time to grieve and express your anger. Thus, the first step to healing is to recognize the betrayal and your emotions rather than contemplating retaliation because of the anger, grief, and humiliation. Take time to examine the betrayal and the relationship because it involves a life-changing decision. Also, discuss the betrayal with the betrayer with a view to discovering the reason behind the betrayal and resolving the issue. Learn to forgive because it is a sure way of taking responsibility for your own happiness. Do not blame yourself and detach from people you do not trust.

Another significant aspect of the healing process is rebuilding of trust which entails forgiving the betrayer by making a conscious effort to love while letting go of the past. Bear with each other and forgive one another if any of you has a grievance against someone. Forgive as the Lord forgave you (Colossians 3:13). Let go of all resentments by not ruminating or pondering over the betrayal again and again because it can deny you the opportunity to experience joy. Forgiveness does not mean excusing or accepting the betrayal, but it helps you to free yourself from the anguish, grudge, and anger towards the betrayer. No relationship, especially within any type of family, can be sustained without forgiveness. It involves a deliberate decision to put the betrayal behind you and chart a new course in your relationship with the betrayer. In extreme cases, you may need to cut ties with the betrayer, especially if such person is a repeat offender to prevent a caustic relationship that could damage your health. If it be possible, as much as lieth in you, live peaceably with all men (Romans 12: 18). The Biblical injunction for us to live peaceably with all men is predicated on two conditions. The first condition is for you to determine the possibility of leaving peaceably with a person. The second condition further establish that the onus of determining such possibility rests with the person being betrayed because he who wears the shoes knows where it pinches.

The last but not the least in the healing process is cultivating an attitude of gratitude. The Bible enjoins us to give thanks in all things and for all things and those things sure include a betrayal. In everything give thanks; for this is the will of God in Christ Jesus concerning you (1 Thessalonians 5:18). Feeling and expressing gratitude can make you healthier and live longer. It reduces stress and increases emotional resilience. It also helps you sleep better and can boosts your immune system. The benefits of being grateful include opening the door to more and better relationships; improvement in physical and psychological health; enhancement of empathy and reduction of aggression; as well as improvement of self-esteem and increasing of mental strength. You can cultivate an attitude of gratitude by writing down what you are grateful for despite the betrayal or keeping a gratitude journal. You can also share what you are thankful for, meditate on it regularly, and express what you are grateful for. Gratitude is a positive emotion that helps us to focus on good things in our lives and be thankful for the things we have. Gratitude is pausing to notice and appreciate the things that we often take for granted, including some virtues in the life of the betrayer.

I have no hesitation to recommend this gem for your reading pleasure. I am also convinced that the lived experience of the author will help you to handle a betrayal from your families and loved ones.

Adebamiji Kunle Olulowo, PhD

CHAPTER 1
WHAT IS FAMILY?

Family as defined in the Bible

The concept of family is extremely important in the Bible, both in a physical sense and in a theological sense. It was introduced in the very beginning, as we see in Genesis 1:28, "God blessed them and said to them, 'Be fruitful and increase in number; fill the earth and subdue it. Rule over the fish of the sea and the birds of the air and over every living creature that moves on the ground.'" God's plan for creation was for men and women to marry and have children. A man and a woman would form a "one-flesh" union through marriage (Genesis 2:24), and they with their children become a family, the essential building block of human society.

The importance of family can be seen in the provisions of the Mosaic covenant. For example, two of the Ten Commandments deal with maintaining the cohesiveness of the family. The fifth commandment regarding honoring parents is meant to preserve the authority of parents in family matters, while the seventh commandment prohibiting adultery protects the sanctity of marriage. From the two flow all the various other stipulations in the Mosaic Law, which seeks to protect marriage and the family. The health of the family was so important to God that it was codified in the national covenant of Israel.

The physical family is the most important building block to human society, and as such, it should be nurtured and protected. But more important than that is the new creation that God is making in Christ, which is the spiritual family, the Church, made up of all people who call upon the Lord Jesus Christ as Savior. This is a family drawn "from every nation, tribe, people and language" (Revelation 7:9), and the defining characteristic of this spiritual family is love for one another: "A new command I give you: Love one another. As I have loved you, so you must love one another. By this all men will know that you are my disciples, if you love one another" (John 13:34-35).

Family as defined in the African culture

The concept of family is one of universal precedence amongst all Africans, whether they belong to the west, east, central or southern regions. The dynamics of an African family is a vital aspect of African livelihood. It is what unifies us. It has been said that family is the foundation on which our society is built and is proven by the fact that all over the world, every society is structured around a family unit. Growing up in Akum Village in Cameroon near the West Coast of Central Africa, family was everything and included more people than DNA (deoxyribonucleic acid, the carrier of genetic information, a self-replicating material which is present in nearly all living organisms as the main constituent of chromosomes) could ever connect. Even the reverend sisters and fathers from Ireland, England and Germany working as missionaries in Akum village were also considered family.

Family as defined by sociology

Sociologists identify different types of families based on how one enters them. A family of orientation refers to the family into which a person is born. A family of procreation describes one that is formed through marriage. These distinctions have cultural significance related to issues of lineage.

Family through the process of adoption

In adoption, a person assumes the parenting of another, usually a child, from that person's biological or legal parent or parents. Legal adoptions permanently transfer all rights and responsibilities, along with filiation, from the biological parent or parents. Historically, some societies have enacted specific laws governing adoption, where others have tried to achieve adoption through less formal means, notably via contracts that specified inheritance rights and parental responsibilities without an accompanying transfer of filiation. Modern systems of adoption, arising in the 20th century, tend to be governed by comprehensive statutes and regulations.

> *"Bear with each other and forgive one another if any of you has a grievance against someone. Forgive as the Lord forgave you."*
>
> *Colossians 3:13*

CHAPTER 2
WHAT IS FAMILY LOYALTY?

Family loyalty refers to the **feelings of mutual obligation, commitment and closeness that exist among family members** (e.g., parents and children, grandparents and grandchildren, siblings). Solidarity is an indicator of family loyalty. Family loyalty is defined primarily in two different ways: (1) adherence to norms of filial obligation; and (2) the level of intergenerational solidarity or closeness between the generations in a family. Loyalty is essential for genuine family solidarity. But blind loyalty leads to family dysfunction. A loyal family member is faithful to the family's traditions and honors its obligations.

A loyal family member is emotionally present with support and encouragement during success or duress. These unwavering devotions are admirable and observable: just look at how a loyal family member helps another member during an illness, a financial crisis, the breakup of a marriage, or death. Remember, there is no shame in admitting that we have wounds from some family experiences and that we have wounded others, sometimes blindly so, but let's not make blind loyalty into a family affair. Instead, let's accept that no family is perfect, and most do the best they can. When we are open to this conscious shift from being a blindly loyal family member to an authentically loyal family member, our families will be true places of refuge. Places where we can always return to heal a hurt, to laugh and cry. Family loyalty is behavior in which you stay firm in your friendship or support for someone in the family. Loyalty is not a word — it's a lifestyle. There's something wrong with your character if opportunity controls your loyalty. True loyalty will result in actions.

What the Bible says about God's promises

- **Ephesians 6:10-18:** Finally, be strong in the LORD and in his mighty power. Put on the full armor of God, so that you can take your stand against the devil's schemes. For our struggle is not against flesh and blood, but against the rulers, against the authorities, against the powers of this dark world and against the spiritual forces of evil in the heavenly realms. Therefore, put on the full armor of God, so that when the day of evil comes, you may be able to stand your ground, and after you have done everything, to stand. Stand firm then, with the belt of truth buckled around your waist, with the breastplate of righteousness in place, and with your feet fitted with the readiness that comes from the gospel of peace. In addition to all this, take up the shield of faith, with which you can extinguish all the flaming arrows of the evil one. Take the helmet of salvation and the sword of the Spirit, which is the word of God. And pray in the Spirit on all occasions with all kinds of prayers and requests. Be alert and always keep on praying for all the LORD's people.

- **Ephesians 6:4:** Fathers, do not provoke your children to anger, but bring them up in the discipline and instruction of the Lord.
- **Genesis 2:24:** Therefore, a man shall leave his father and his mother and hold fast to his wife, and they shall become one flesh.
- **Genesis 12:3:** I will bless those who bless you, and whoever curses you I will curse; and all peoples on earth will be blessed through you.
- **Proverbs 21:21:** He who pursues righteousness and loyalty finds life, righteousness and honor.

"Bear with each other and forgive one another if any of you has a grievance against someone. Forgive as the Lord forgave you."

Colossians 3:13

CHAPTER 3
WHAT IS FAMILY BETRAYAL?

Family betrayal is a violation or breaking of a trust, contract, or confidence between individuals in a family. You want to believe that there's one relationship in life that's beyond betrayal, a relationship that's beyond that kind of hurt, but there isn't. We get so wrapped up into the mentality that family sticks together no matter what, thus allowing family members closest to us to give us the most grief and pain because, well, *"family is forever"*.

Family betrayal is emotionally heavy. Dealing with feelings of betrayal has a lot to do with the closeness of that family member and the level of trust that was broken. Sometimes, family members do unpredictable things. For there to be betrayal, there would have to have been trust first. Sometimes, the only defense we have after family betrayal is to distrust each other. Family betrayal is never easy to handle and there is no right way to accept it. As much as you may want to love all of your family members and wish the best for all of them, when they betray you and you finally gather the guts to take a step back, you may be shocked! You may actually realize that some of the family members you have loved, trusted and nurtured are the same ones that would happily find your shortcomings, ignore your great achievements, recruit other family members to join them in betraying you even more.

Family isn't just a bloodline, one-sided trust and loyalty or last name. Family should be unconditional love and trust, crowned with unwavering loyalty. Always remember that not all family members want to see you succeed and not all family members will be loyal. Though you cannot choose your bloodline family, it's great to look around and feel the warmth of the people God has allowed into your life, without your permission or through marriage. Family is defined by love, support, honesty, loyalty, bond, forgiveness, tolerance, celebrating and inspiring each other. The family prayer should be godly success for all, and God's plan accomplished in all.

What the Bible says about betrayal

- **Mark 13:12:** And brother will deliver brother over to death, and the father his child, and children will rise against parents and have them put to death.
- **Matthew 24:10:** And then many will fall away and betray one another and hate one another.
- **Matthew 10:21:** Brother will deliver brother over to death, and the father his child, and children will rise against parents and have them put to death,
- **Luke 21:16:** You will be delivered up even by parents and brothers and relatives and friends, and some of you they will put to death.
- **Luke 12:53:** They will be divided, father against son and son against father, mother against daughter and daughter against mother, mother-in-law against her

daughter-in-law and daughter-in-law against mother-in-law.

- **Luke 12:51-53:** Do you think that I have come to give peace on earth? No, I tell you, but rather division. For from now on, in one house, there will be five divided, three against two and two against three. They will be divided, father against son and son against father, mother against daughter and daughter against mother, mother-in-law against her daughter-in-law and daughter-in-law against mother-in-law.

- **Matthew 10:35-36:** For I have come to set a man against his father, and a daughter against her mother, and a daughter-in-law against her mother-in-law. And a person's enemies will be those of his own household.

- **2 Timothy 3:1-5:** But mark this: There will be terrible times in the last days. People will be lovers of themselves, lovers of money, boastful, proud, abusive, disobedient to their parents, ungrateful, unholy, without love, unforgiving, slanderous, without self-control, brutal, not lovers of the good, treacherous, rash, conceited, lovers of pleasure rather than lovers of God- having a form of godliness but denying its power. Have nothing to do with such people.

- **Proverbs 19:5:** A false witness will not go unpunished, and whoever pours out lies will not go free.

- **Psalm 12:1-2:** Help, LORD, for no one is faithful anymore; those who are loyal have vanished from humanity. Everyone lies to their neighbor; they flatter with their lips but harbor deception in their hearts.

✟ **Matthew 6:14-15:** For if you forgive other people when they sin against you, your heavenly Father will also forgive you. But if you do not forgive others their sins, your Father will not forgive your sins.

....

"Bear with each other and forgive one another if any of you has a grievance against someone. Forgive as the Lord forgave you."
Colossians 3:13

....

CHAPTER 4
CAIN AND ABEL: THE FIRST FAMILY BETRAYAL

Genesis 4:1-16 tells the story of Cain and Abel, the sons of Adam and Eve. Cain, the firstborn, was a farmer, and his brother Abel was a shepherd. Abel greatly loved Cain, but Cain did not feel the same way. Cain had no great will to work. Abel, on the contrary, was greatly disposed to labor because he had found it profitable. He was industrious and eventually became a shepherd. The brothers made sacrifices to God, each of his own produce, but God favored Abel's sacrifice instead of Cain's. Cain then murdered Abel, whereupon God punished Cain to a life of wandering. Cain then dwelt in the land of Nod, where he built a city and fathered the line of descendants beginning with Enoch.

Though Cain and Abel both offered sacrifices to God, Abel offered a more excellent sacrifice. An excellent sacrifice is a sacrifice that is joyful, consistent, of best quality, and given with expectations of Godly favor, testimony, and impact.

Lessons to learn from the story of Cain and Abel

- Our deeds are an outward physical statement of our inward self.

- Family is not always forever; you may have to say goodbye to toxic family members to *save* your future.
- Punishment does not mean repentance.
- Life is not a game; don't play with the Cains in your family.
- Don't make your decisions to be more important than the consequences of that decision.
- Your decision may last a minute, but the consequences of that one-minute decision may last forever.

What the Bible says about God's promises

- **Mark 13:12:** And brother will deliver brother over to death, and the father his child, and children will rise against parents and have them put to death.
- **Matthew 24:10:** And then many will fall away and betray one another and hate one another.
- **Psalm 50:15:** And call on me in the day of trouble; I will deliver you, and you will honor Me.
- **Matthew 10:21:** Brother will deliver brother over to death, and the father his child, and children will rise against parents and have them put to death,
- **Luke 21:16:** You will be delivered up even by parents and brothers and relatives and friends, and some of you they will put to death.
- **Luke 12:53:** They will be divided, father against son and son against father, mother against daughter and daughter against mother, mother-in-law against her daughter-in-law and daughter-in-law against mother-in-law.

⚔ **Luke 12:51-53:** Do you think that I have come to give peace on earth? No, I tell you, but rather division. For from now on, in one house, there will be five divided, three against two and two against three. They will be divided, father against son and son against father, mother against daughter and daughter against mother, mother-in-law against her daughter-in-law and daughter-in-law against mother-in-law.

⚔ **Matthew 10:35-36:** For I have come to set a man against his father, and a daughter against her mother, and a daughter-in-law against her mother-in-law. And a person's enemies will be those of his own household.

⚔ **2 Timothy 3:1-5:** But mark this: There will be terrible times in the last days. People will be lovers of themselves, lovers of money, boastful, proud, abusive, disobedient to their parents, ungrateful, unholy, without love, unforgiving, slanderous, without self-control, brutal, not lovers of the good, treacherous, rash, conceited, lovers of pleasure rather than lovers of God, having a form of godliness but denying its power. Have nothing to do with such people.

....

"Bear with each other and forgive one another if any of you has a grievance against someone. Forgive as the Lord forgave you."

Colossians 3:13

....

CHAPTER 5
THE BETRAYAL OF JOSEPH BY HIS BROTHERS

Joseph was the 11th son of Jacob. As a 17-year-old shepherd, Joseph is somewhat of a tattletale, bringing a bad report about his brothers to their father (*Genesis 37:2*). This behavior, combined with Jacob's overt favoritism towards Joseph, causes his older brothers to resent him to the point of hatred (*Genesis 37:3-4*). Because of Jacob's open love for Joseph, his favoritism was begrudged by his other sons.

And when Jacob presented Joseph with a highly decorated coat, he was hated and resented by his brothers even more (*Genesis 37:3*). To make matters worse, Joseph begins relating his dreams — prophetic visions showing him one day ruling over his family (*Genesis 37:11-15*). The animosity towards Joseph peaks when his brothers plot to kill him in the wilderness. Reuben, the eldest, objects to outright murder, so instead, the brothers sell Joseph as a slave and deceive their father into thinking his favorite son had been slain by wild beasts (*Genesis 37:18-35).*

What made Joseph different from the rest of his siblings

1. He was a special child given birth in answer to a long time of prayer. *Then God remembered Rachel, and God listened to her and opened her womb.* Genesis 30:22

2. He took away the reproach of barrenness on Rachel. **Genesis 30:23**: And she conceived and bore a son, and said, "God has taken away my reproach.
3. He was more righteous than his brothers, refused to participate or join them in evil. **Genesis 37:2**: This is the history of Jacob. Joseph, being seventeen years old, was feeding the flock with his brothers. And the lad was with the sons of Bilhah and the sons of Zilpah, his father's wives; and Joseph brought a bad report of them to his father.
4. His father loved him. He was the son of Jacob's old age. **Genesis 37:3**: Now Israel loved Joseph more than all his children, because he was the son of his old age. Also, he made him a tunic of many colors.
5. He had a divine gift of interpreting dreams. **Genesis 37:5**: Now Joseph had a dream, and he told it to his brothers; and they hated him even more. **Genesis 40:8**: And they said to him, "We each have had a dream, and there is no interpreter of it."
6. He loved his brothers, but his brothers hated him. **Genesis 37:5**: Now Joseph had a dream, and he told it to his brothers; and they hated him even more.
7. He was a prophet. **Genesis 37: 7, 9**: There we were, binding sheaves in the field. Then behold, my sheaf arose and also stood upright; and indeed, your sheaves stood all around and bowed down to my sheaf." Then he dreamed still another dream and told it to his brothers, and said, "Look, I have dreamed another dream. And this time, the sun, the moon, and the eleven stars bowed down to me."

8. He was envied by his brothers because of the gift of God in his life. **Genesis 37:11**: And his brothers envied him, but his father kept the matter in mind.

9. He was hardworking, persistent and did not give up easily. **Genesis 37: 15-18**: Now a certain man found him, and there he was, wandering in the field. And the man asked him, saying, "What are you seeking?" So, he said, "I am seeking my brothers. Please tell me where they are feeding their flocks." And the man said, "They have departed from here, for I heard them say, 'Let us go to Dothan.'" So, Joseph went after his brothers and found them in Dothan. Now when they saw him afar off, even before he came near them, they conspired against him to kill him.

10. He was favored by God. **Genesis 39: 3,21**: And his master saw that the Lord was with him and that the Lord made all he did to prosper in his hand. But the Lord was with Joseph and showed him mercy, and He gave him favor in the sight of the keeper of the prison.

11. Even as a slave, he was very prosperous.

12. God's presence was with him in Potiphar's house. **Genesis 39: 2**: The Lord was with Joseph, and he was a successful man; and he was in the house of his master the Egyptian. **Genesis 39:23:** The keeper of the prison did not look into anything that was under Joseph's authority because the Lord was with him and whatever he did, the Lord made it prosper.

Lessons to learn from Joseph's betrayal

- **Genesis 41:38-49:** When all was said and done, Joseph was made a ruler in Egypt, second only to the king at the age of 30.
- After all Josephs ordeals, Joseph can see God's hand at work.
- **Genesis 45:5:** Now therefore be not grieved, nor angry with yourselves, that ye sold me hither: for God did send me before you to preserve life.
- **Genesis 45:7-8:** And God sent me before you to preserve you a posterity in the earth, and to save your lives by a great deliverance. So now it was not you that sent me hither, but God: and he hath made me a father to Pharaoh, and lord of all his house, and a ruler throughout all the land of Egypt.
- **Genesis 50:20**: But as for you, ye thought evil against me; but God meant it unto good, to bring to pass, as it is this day, to save much people alive.
- Man's most wicked intentions can never thwart the perfect plan of God.
- Sometimes in life, God doesn't require you to defeat your enemies, but He expects you to outlast their opposition to get to your godly ordained destiny. Embrace the stubborn faith of Joseph. He outlasted the opposition of his brothers.

What the Bible says about betrayal

- **Mark 13:12:** And brother will deliver brother over to death, and the father his child, and children will rise against parents and have them put to death.

- **Matthew 24:10:** And then many will fall away and betray one another and hate one another.

- **Matthew 10:21:** Brother will deliver brother over to death, and the father his child, and children will rise against parents and have them put to death.

- **Luke 21:16:** You will be delivered up even by parents and brothers and relatives and friends, and some of you they will put to death.

- **Luke 12:53:** They will be divided, father against son and son against father, mother against daughter and daughter against mother, mother-in-law against her daughter-in-law and daughter-in-law against mother-in-law.

- **Luke 12:51-53:** Do you think that I have come to give peace on earth? No, I tell you, but rather division. For from now on in one house there will be five divided, three against two and two against three. They will be divided, father against son and son against father, mother against daughter and daughter against mother, mother-in-law against her daughter-in-law and daughter-in-law against mother-in-law.

- **Matthew 10:35-36:** For I have come to set a man against his father, and a daughter against her mother, and a daughter-in-law against her mother-in-law. And a person's enemies will be those of his own household.

⚠ **2 Timothy 3:1-5:** But mark this: There will be terrible times in the last days. People will be lovers of themselves, lovers of money, boastful, proud, abusive, disobedient to their parents, ungrateful, unholy, without love, unforgiving, slanderous, without self-control, brutal, not lovers of the good, treacherous, rash, conceited, lovers of pleasure rather than lovers of God, having a form of godliness but denying its power. Have nothing to do with such people.

"Bear with each other and forgive one another if any of you has a grievance against someone. Forgive as the Lord forgave you."
Colossians 3:13

CHAPTER 6
THE BETRAYAL OF ESAU BY HIS BROTHER JACOB AND HIS MOTHER REBECCA

Genesis 27 (NIV)

When Isaac was old and his eyes were so weak that he could no longer see, he called for Esau his older son and said to him, "My son." "Here I am," he answered. Isaac said, "I am now an old man and don't know the day of my death. Now then, get your equipment—your quiver and bow—and go out to the open country to hunt some wild game for me. Prepare me the kind of tasty food I like and bring it to me to eat, so that I may give you my blessing before I die." Now Rebekah was listening as Isaac spoke to his son Esau.

When Esau left for the open country to hunt game and bring it back, Rebekah said to her son Jacob, "Look, I overheard your father say to your brother Esau, 'Bring me some game and prepare me some tasty food to eat, so that I may give you my blessing in the presence of the Lord before I die.' Now, my son, listen carefully and do what I tell you: Go out to the flock and bring me two choice young goats, so I can prepare some tasty food for your father, just the way he likes it. Then take it to your father to eat, so that he may give you his blessing before he dies." Jacob said to Rebekah his mother, "But my brother Esau is a hairy man while I have smooth skin. What if my father touches me? I would appear to be tricking him and would bring down a curse on myself rather than a blessing." His mother said to him, "My son, let the curse fall on me. Just do what I say, go and get them for me." So, he went and got them and brought them to his mother, and she prepared some tasty food, just the way his father liked it. Then Rebekah took the best clothes of Esau her older son, which she had in the house, and put them on her younger son Jacob. She also covered his hands and the smooth part of his neck with the goatskins. Then she handed to her son Jacob the tasty food and the bread she had made. He went to his father and said, "My father." "Yes, my son," he answered. "Who is it?" Jacob said to his father, "I am Esau your firstborn. I have done as you told me. Please sit up and eat some of my game, so that you may give me your blessing." Isaac asked his son, "How did you find it so quickly, my son?"

"The Lord your God gave me success," he replied. Then Isaac said to Jacob, "Come near so I can touch you, my son, to know whether you really are my son Esau or not." Jacob went close to his father Isaac, who touched him and said, "The voice is the voice of Jacob, but the hands are the hands of Esau." He did not recognize him, for his hands were hairy like those of his brother Esau; so, he proceeded to bless him. "Are you really my son Esau?" he asked. "I am," he replied. Then he said, "My son, bring me some of your game to eat, so that I may give you my blessing."

Jacob brought it to him, and he ate; and he brought some wine and he drank. Then his father Isaac said to him, "Come here, my son, and kiss me."

So, he went to him and kissed him. When Isaac caught the smell of his clothes, he blessed him and said, "Ah, the smell of my son is like the smell of a field that the Lord has blessed. May God give you heaven's dew and earth's richness— an abundance of grain and new wine. May nations serve you and peoples bow down to you. Be lord over your brothers and may the sons of your mother bow down to you. May those who curse you be cursed and those who bless you be blessed."

After Isaac finished blessing him, and Jacob had scarcely left his father's presence, his brother Esau came in from hunting. He too prepared some tasty food and brought it to his father. Then he said to him, "My father, please sit up and eat some of my game, so that you may give me your blessing." His father Isaac asked him, "Who are you?" "I am your son," he answered, "your firstborn, Esau." Isaac trembled violently and said, "Who was it, then, that hunted game and brought it to me? I ate it just before you came, and I blessed him—and indeed he will be blessed!"

When Esau heard his father's words, he burst out with a loud and bitter cry and said to his father, "Bless me—me too, my father!" But he said, "Your brother came deceitfully and took your blessing." Esau said, "Isn't he rightly named Jacob? This is the second time he has taken advantage of me: He took my birthright, and now he's taken my blessing!" Then he asked, "Haven't you reserved any blessing for me?". Isaac answered Esau, "I have made him lord over you and have made all his relatives his servants, and I have sustained him with grain and new wine. So, what can I possibly do for you, my son?" Esau said to his father, "Do you have only one blessing, my father? Bless me, too, my father!" Then Esau wept aloud. His father Isaac answered him, "Your dwelling will be away from the earth's richness, away from the dew of heaven above. You will live by the sword and you will serve your brother. But when you grow restless, you will throw his yoke from off your neck."

Esau held a grudge against Jacob because of the blessing his father had given him. He said to himself, "The days of mourning for my father are near; then I will kill my brother Jacob." When Rebekah was told what her older son Esau had said, she sent for her younger son Jacob and said to him, "Your brother Esau is planning to avenge himself by killing you. Now then, my son, do what I say: Flee at once to my brother Laban in Harran. Stay with him for a while until your brother's fury subsides. When your brother is no longer angry with you and forgets what you did to him, I'll send word for you to come back from there. Why should I lose both of you in one day?" Then Rebekah said to Isaac, "I'm disgusted with living because of these Hittite women. If Jacob takes a wife from among the women of this land, from Hittite women like these, my life will not be worth living."

Lessons to learn from Esau's betrayal

- A parent's unreasonable decision to favor one child over the other child can erupt into a dangerous feud between two children.
- Insights about character and personal growth are displayed in this story of betrayal.

- There is hope for flawed people such as Jacob because God's choice to bless us is based on His purposes, not ours.
- Entrust yourself to God and let Him take care of your heart and the heart of your betrayer.
- The virtue of forgiveness comes only on the heels of hurt and betrayal and the ability to accept others is manifest only when we meet those who challenge or even repel us.
- Forgive, but don't give your betrayer other opportunities to hurt you.
- Revenge belongs to God. If it is possible, as far as it depends on you, live at peace with everyone. Do not take revenge, my dear friends, but leave room for God's wrath, for it is written: "It is mine to avenge; I will repay," says the Lord (Romans 12:18-19).

What the Bible says about betrayal

- **Mark 13:12:** And brother will deliver brother over to death, and the father his child, and children will rise against parents and have them put to death.
- **Matthew 24:10:** And then many will fall away and betray one another and hate one another.
- **Matthew 10:21:** Brother will deliver brother over to death, and the father his child, and children will rise against parents and have them put to death.

- **Luke 21:16:** You will be delivered up even by parents and brothers and relatives and friends, and some of you they will put to death.
- **Luke 12:53:** They will be divided, father against son and son against father, mother against daughter and daughter against mother, mother-in-law against her daughter-in-law and daughter-in-law against mother-in-law.
- **Luke 12:51-53:** Do you think that I have come to give peace on earth? No, I tell you, but rather division. For from now on, in one house, there will be five divided, three against two and two against three. They will be divided, father against son and son against father, mother against daughter and daughter against mother, mother-in-law against her daughter-in-law and daughter-in-law against mother-in-law.
- **Matthew 10:35-36:** For I have come to set a man against his father, and a daughter against her mother, and a daughter-in-law against her mother-in-law. And a person's enemies will be those of his own household.

....

"Bear with each other and forgive one another if any of you has a grievance against someone. Forgive as the Lord forgave you."

Colossians 3:13

....

CHAPTER 7
INVASION OF PRIVACY: A SHAMEFUL SECRET BEHIND FAMILY BETRAYALS

An invasion of privacy occurs when there is an intrusion upon your reasonable expectation to be left alone. Privacy is a basic human need, and invasion of privacy can have serious psychological and emotional consequences, including paranoia, anxiety, depression, and broken trust. It is an area of growing concern in most families at this age of technological advancement.

Children require appropriate amounts of privacy and autonomy to develop into mature, independently minded members of the family and community. Privacy is what allows us to determine who we are and who we want to be, but these days, kids can't even get such privacy in their own homes. Technological advancements over the last decade have provided parents with tools that were formerly available only to law enforcement and government: software that monitors online and mobile communication; GPS tracking devices that can be strapped to backpacks and wrists; even palm scanners in cafeterias to monitor caloric intake. Security cameras have become commonplace in schools, malls and other public places for decades, leaving the family home as the last bastion of youth privacy. Unfortunately, the use of in-home cameras is widespread and growing. The invasion of the privacy of children by parents is no doubt an ultimate shameful secret behind family betrayals in the modern family.

Invasion of privacy is both a legal and an ethical issue. The four main types of invasion of privacy claims according to FindLaw's team of legal writers and editors are:

1. **Intrusion of Solitude.** Someone illegally intercepting private phone calls or snooping through someone's private records.
2. **Appropriation of Name or Likeness**. This happens when someone used your name or likeness to his or her benefit without your permission.
3. **Public Disclosure of Private Facts**. This occurs when an individual publicly reveals truthful information that is not of public concern and which a reasonable person would find offensive if made public.
4. **False Light.** The public disclosure of information that is misleading (or puts a person in a "false light"), but not technically false. Generally, a false light claim must contain the following elements: (a) the defendant made a publication about the plaintiff; (b) it was done with reckless disregard; (c) it placed the plaintiff in a false light; and (d) it would be highly offensive or embarrassing to a reasonable person.

Do you have a tracking device in your family member's car or phone to secretly know what they are up to?

Do you have a private investigator following a family member around to catch him or her in the act?

Do you secretly access your family member's emails to see what they're up to?

Do you secretly follow your family member around to know what they're doing and who they are doing it with?

Have you publicly disclosed information that is not of public concern or misleading about your family member?

Have you used your family member's name to your benefit without that family member's knowledge?

Are you illegally intercepting private phone calls, or snooping through your family member's private records?

What the Bible says about invasion of privacy and betrayal

- **Genesis 9: 20-27**: The curse of Ham (placed upon Ham's son Canaan) occurs in the Book of Genesis, imposed by the patriarch Noah. It occurs in the context of Noah's drunkenness and is provoked by a shameful act perpetrated by Noah's son Ham, who "saw the nakedness of his father".
- Invasion of privacy according to the lesson behind Noah's betrayal of his father Ham gets you cursed, and your whole family cursed, for generations to come.

- **Deuteronomy 29:29**: The secret things belong to the Lord our God, but the things revealed belong to us and to our children forever, that we may follow all the words of this law.

- **1 Timothy 5:13-14:** Besides that, they learn to be idlers, going about from house to house, and not only idlers, but also gossips and busybodies, saying what they should not. Find something profitable to do.

- **Mark 13:12:** And brother will deliver brother over to death, and the father his child, and children will rise against parents and have them put to death.

- **Matthew 24:10:** And then many will fall away and betray one another and hate one another.

- **Matthew 10:21:** Brother will deliver brother over to death, and the father his child, and children will rise against parents and have them put to death.

- **Luke 21:16:** You will be delivered up even by parents and brothers and relatives and friends, and some of you they will put to death.

- **Luke 12:53:** They will be divided, father against son and son against father, mother against daughter and daughter against mother, mother-in-law against her daughter-in-law and daughter-in-law against mother-in-law.

- **Luke 12:51-53:** Do you think that I have come to give peace on earth? No, I tell you, but rather division. For from now on in one house there will be five divided, three against two and two against three. They will be divided, father against son and son against father, mother against daughter and daughter against mother, mother-in-law against her daughter-in-law and daughter-in-law against mother-in-law.

- **Matthew 10:35-36:** For I have come to set a man against his father, and a daughter against her mother, and a daughter-in-law against her mother-in-law. And a person's enemies will be those of his own household.

What others say about privacy

- **Gabriel García Márquez:** All human beings have three lives: public, private, and secret.
- **C.S. Lewis:** We live, in fact, in a world starved for solitude, silence, and private: and therefore, starved for meditation and true friendship.
- **David Sedaris:** If you read someone else's diary, you get what you deserve.
- **Henry Giroux:** The social media not only become new platforms for the invasion of privacy, but further legitimate a culture in which monitoring functions are viewed as benign while the state-sponsored society of hyper-fear increasingly defines everyone as either a snitch or a terrorist.

"Bear with each other and forgive one another if any of you has a grievance against someone. Forgive as the Lord forgave you."

Colossians 3:13

CHAPTER 8
LACK OF PRAYERS: A SHAMEFUL SECRET BEHIND FAMILY BETRAYALS

Lack of prayers in a family can no doubt be the shameful secret behind many betrayals in the family. When we fail to pray, we fail at many other things, including family relationships. Not praying can make us anxious, restless, and worried. Growing up in Akum village, the first song about prayer I was taught as a child had the following lyrics *"Prayer is the key, prayer is the key, prayer is the master key, Jesus started with prayer and ended with prayer, prayer is the master key."* The Holy Bible discloses various styles of prayers and uses an array of words to describe the practice. In the first Pastoral Epistle, Paul the Apostle writes to Timothy, his younger colleague and church leader, regarding his ministry in Ephesus saying, "First of all, then, I urge that *supplications, prayers, intercessions,* and *thanksgivings* be made for all people." (1 Timothy 2:1).

What is prayer?

1. Prayer is talking to God. It is our way of communicating our thoughts, needs, and desires to our heavenly father.

2. Prayer is spiritual communication between man and God, a two-way relationship in which man should not only talk to God but also listen to Him.

3. Prayer is an invocation or act that seeks to activate a rapport with God almighty through deliberate communication.

4. Prayer is a divinely inspired restraining order against the enemies

5. Through prayer we can draw closer to God.

6. Prayer means believing in God for what we say with our tongue, what we sincerely feel in our heart, and what we do with our limbs.

7. Prayer helps us build a relationship with God. So, start praying with gratitude and include a song of praise every now and then.

8. Something happens when you pray, and it only happens when you pray

9. You don't learn how to pray by reading a book, you learn how to pray by praying. Follow the example of Jesus Christ and pray according to the knowledge of God and His truths (John 4:24).

10. The power of kneeling before God when you pray shows our dependence upon God. It is a sign of honor to God and our humility.

11. Prayer has the unique ability to replace fear, worry, anxiety with zeal, passion, and enthusiasm when you pray without ceasing.

12. Pray without ceasing by incorporating prayer into your everyday Agenda.
13. Always remember that whenever you pray, God listens and hears you.

A family that prays together stays together. Husbands should pray daily for their wives. Wives should pray daily for their husbands. Parents must pray daily with and for their children. Children should pray daily for their siblings and their parents. Everyone should pray daily for guidance for themselves and others. It is an honor to God and very beneficial to the family unit when families read the Bible together, sing songs to God together, pray together, and tell others of God's love together.

What the Bible says about praying

- **Ephesians 6:18**: And pray in the Spirit on all occasions with all kinds of prayers and requests. With this in mind, be alert and always keep on praying for all the LORD's people. (NIV)
- **1 Thessalonians 5:17:** Pray continually. (NIV)
- **Philippians 4:6:** Do not be anxious about anything, but in every situation, by prayer and petition, with thanksgiving, present your requests to God. (NIV)
- **Matthew 6:5-8:** And when you pray, do not be like the hypocrites, for they love to pray standing in the synagogues and on the street corners to be seen by others. Truly I tell you, they have received their reward in full. But when you pray, go into your room,

close the door and pray to your Father, who is unseen. Then your Father, who sees what is done in secret, will reward you. And when you pray, do not keep on babbling like pagans, for they think they will be heard because of their many words. Do not be like them, for your Father knows what you need before you ask him. (NIV)

▲ **Psalm 50:15:** And call on me in the day of trouble; I will deliver you, and you will honor me.

"Bear with each other and forgive one another if any of you has a grievance against someone. Forgive as the Lord forgave you."

Colossians 3:13

CHAPTER 9
FAMILY JEALOUSY: A SHAMEFUL SECRET BEHIND FAMILY BETRAYALS

Jealousy generally refers to the thoughts or feelings of insecurity, fear, and concern over a relative lack of possessions. It can consist of one or more emotions, such as anger, resentment, inadequacy, helplessness, or disgust. A common family relationship problem is jealousy from other family members. The division that it causes is undeniable. Jealous family members can be toxic and cause a lot of stress on you. Their jealousy, and other negative traits can drain you emotionally and make you feel bad about yourself. All these things affect your health both directly and indirectly. A jealous family member will seldom be happy for you. She will hardly celebrate your successes, and It will take a lot of prompting for her to compliment or congratulate you. The more you succeed, the more your jealous family member starts distancing themselves from you. They start feeling like victims in life and verbalizing it to you. They start gossiping negative things about you to other family members

When something bad happens to you, however, the jealous family member will be there with bells on and nonstop prayers and swoop in with false sympathy. And when God who sees all and knows all finally delivers you from your ordeal, your jealous family member will make it a point of claiming that her prayers took you right out of the grave back to life. There will never be any true empathy, compassion, comfort, or encouragement. Jealous family members have the following in common:

- ▲ They never seem to be impressed with your accomplishments; instead, they try to outdo you.
- ▲ When you reach a milestone yet again, most of their conversations are characterized by anger, rage and an inability to talk calmly.
- ▲ They talk negatively about you behind your back with other family members
- ▲ The atmosphere around jealous family members is usually tense, causing feelings of irritability.
- ▲ Jealous family members will go out of their way to mention people who are "better" than you and will get angry when you offer advice.

Lessons to learn from family jealousy

- ▲ Family as God's ideal institution is supposed to be a cure of society's social, emotional, phycological and spiritual ills (Dr. Myles Munroe)
- ▲ Family jealousy is the ultimate and shameful secret behind many family abuse and betrayal cases
- ▲ The ugliest jealousy of all is when a parent is jealous of their own child
- ▲ Jealousy of a parent toward their child is rarely acknowledged. This is one thing that people are very

uncomfortable talking about and few will even admit it exists.

What the Bible says about family jealousy

- **1 Corinthians 3:3:** You are still worldly. For since there is jealousy and quarreling among you, are you not worldly? Are you not acting like mere humans?

- **Proverbs 27:4:** Anger is cruel and fury overwhelming, but who can stand before jealousy?

- **Song of Solomon 8:6:** Place me like a seal over your heart, like a seal on your arm; for love is as strong as death, its jealousy unyielding as the grave. It burns like blazing fire, like a mighty flame.

- **Mark 11:25:** And when you stand praying, if you hold anything against anyone, forgive them, so that your Father in heaven may forgive you your sins.

- **Galatians 5:19-21**: The acts of the flesh are obvious: sexual immorality, impurity and debauchery; idolatry and witchcraft; hatred, discord, jealousy, fits of rage, selfish ambition, dissensions, factions and envy; drunkenness, orgies, and the like. I warn you, as I did before, that those who live like this will not inherit the kingdom of God.

- **James 3:14-16:** But if you harbor bitter envy and selfish ambition in your hearts, do not boast about it or deny the truth. Such "wisdom" does not come down from heaven but is earthly, unspiritual, demonic. For where you have envy and selfish ambition, there you find disorder and every evil practice.

▲ **Romans 12:1-2**: Therefore, I urge you, brothers and sisters, in view of God's mercy, to offer your bodies as a living sacrifice, holy and pleasing to God — this is your true and proper worship. Do not conform to the pattern of this world but be transformed by the renewing of your mind. Then you will be able to test and approve what God's will is — His good, pleasing and perfect will.

"Bear with each other and forgive one another if any of you has a grievance against someone. Forgive as the Lord forgave you."

Colossians 3:13

CHAPTER 10
THE BETRAYAL OF RACHEL BY HER FATHER LABAN AND HER SISTER LEAH

Genesis 29

So, it came about, when Laban heard the news of Jacob, his sister's son, that he ran to meet him, and embraced him and kissed him, and brought him to his house. Then he related to Laban all these things. And Laban said to him, "Surely, you are my bone and my flesh." And he stayed with him a month. Then Laban said to Jacob, "Because you are my relative, should you therefore serve me for nothing? Tell me, what shall your wages be?" Now Laban had two daughters; the name of the older was Leah, and the name of the younger was Rachel. And Leah's eyes were weak, but Rachel was beautiful of form and face. Now Jacob loved Rachel, so he said, "I will serve you seven years for your younger daughter Rachel." And Laban said, "It is better that I give her to you than that I should give her to another man; stay with me." So, Jacob served seven years for Rachel and they seemed to him but a few days because of his love for her. Then Jacob said to Laban, "Give me my wife, for my time is completed, that I may go into her." And Laban gathered all the men of the place and made a feast. Now it came about in the evening that he took his daughter Leah and brought her to him; and Jacob went into her. Laban also gave his maid Zilpah to his daughter Leah as a maid. So, it came about in the morning that, behold, it was Leah! And he said to Laban, "What is this you have done to me? Was it not for Rachel that I served with you? Why then have you deceived me?" But Laban said, "It is not the practice in our place to marry off the younger before the firstborn. Complete the week of this one, and we will give you the other also for the service which you shall serve with me for another seven years." And Jacob did so and completed her week, and he gave him his daughter Rachel as his wife. Laban also gave his maid Bilhah to his daughter Rachel as her maid. So, Jacob went into Rachel also, and indeed he loved Rachel more than Leah, and he served with Laban for another seven years.

Lessons to learn from Rachel's betrayal

- ▲ Marriage is between one man and one woman. Here is what Jesus said when He was questioned about marriage and divorce in Matthew 19:4-6:
- ▲ *"Haven't you read," he replied, "that at the beginning the Creator 'made them male and female,' and said, 'For this reason a man will leave his father and mother and be united to his wife, and the two will become one flesh'? So, they are no longer two, but one flesh. Therefore, what God has joined together, let no one separate."*
- ▲ Women are not to be a man's property based upon their looks; they are to be the living souls that God created them to be.

- Betrayal and incest can never be a part of God's heavenly will.
- God may have chosen the sons of Jacob to lead the 12 tribes of Israel, but it was not because Jacob and his sons were truly righteous; it had more to do with His promise to make a nation of them.

Jacob and his sons failed to follow God's heavenly will. Instead, they compounded betrayal and incest with all the other corrupt ways of this world, including killing one another and mistreating and killing animals, which has continued to this very day. We need to reject these worldly ways and become the peacemaking children of God that Jesus called us to be.

What the Bible says about betrayal

- **Mark 13:12:** And brother will deliver brother over to death, and the father his child, and children will rise against parents and have them put to death.
- **Matthew 24:10:** And then many will fall away and betray one another and hate one another.
- **Matthew 10:21:** Brother will deliver brother over to death, and the father his child, and children will rise against parents and have them put to death.
- **Luke 21:16:** You will be delivered up even by parents and brothers and relatives and friends, and some of you they will put to death.
- **Luke 12:53:** They will be divided, father against son

and son against father, mother against daughter and daughter against mother, mother-in-law against her daughter-in-law and daughter-in-law against mother-in-law.

- **Luke 12:51-53:** Do you think that I have come to give peace on earth? No, I tell you, but rather division. For from now on in one house there will be five divided, three against two and two against three. They will be divided, father against son and son against father, mother against daughter and daughter against mother, mother-in-law against her daughter-in-law and daughter-in-law against mother-in-law.

- **Matthew 10:35-36:** For I have come to set a man against his father, and a daughter against her mother, and a daughter-in-law against her mother-in-law. And a person's enemies will be those of his own household.

"Bear with each other and forgive one another if any of you has a grievance against someone. Forgive as the Lord forgave you."

Colossians 3:13

CHAPTER 11
FAMILY CULTURE: A SHAMEFUL SECRET BEHIND FAMILY BETRAYALS

Family culture refers to the values, rules and traditions that govern a family's life and routine. Every family has its own dynamic: a distinct way of doing things, tackle daily activities, solve common problems, set family goals, and how to relate to one another. The bitter truth is that a family culture is created, whether we intend to or not. Even if we don't make conscious decisions and openly discuss our values, norms and traditions within our household, we still create a family culture. As Roy Disney brilliantly puts it, ***"It's not hard to make decisions when you know what your values are."*** Once a family culture is developed, aligning family and personal decisions and actions with family values can help strengthen family relationships and family bonds.

Couples come from different family cultures with different backgrounds and have certainly been through different experiences. When they get married, they unite to form yet another family culture. The good place to start is by having a common positive and healthy vision even before children get in the picture. ***"Vision unites, gives focus, dominates all inner conversations and inspires greatness"*** **(Miller 1995).** On the other hand, a lack of or having negative common vision will foster strained family relationships and betrayals. A strong family system with assigned roles and responsibilities can help in creating a healthy family culture while uncertainty or dissatisfaction regarding our family roles create disharmony and imbalance in the family system.

- ▲ Do you have a family culture of "Do what I say, not what I do"?
- ▲ Do you have a culture of disrespect in the family?
- ▲ Do you have a family culture of alcohol and drug abuse?
- ▲ Do you have a culture of domestic abuse and violence in your home?

If you answer yes to any of these, it will lead to many betrayals in your family.

What the Bible says about God's promises

- ▲ **Deuteronomy 31:6:** Be strong and courageous. Do not be afraid or terrified because of them, for the LORD your God goes with you; he will never leave you nor forsake you.
- ▲ **Ephesians 3:20:** Now to him who can do immeasurably more than all we ask or imagine, according to his power that is at work within us.
- ▲ **Hebrews 7:25:** Therefore, he can save completely those who come to God through him, because he always lives to intercede for them.
- ▲ **Isaiah 41:10:** So, do not fear, for I am with you; do not be dismayed, for I am your God. I will strengthen

you and help you; I will uphold you with my righteous right hand.

- **Psalm 23:4-6**: Even though I walk through the darkest valley, I will fear no evil, for you are with me; your rod and your staff, they comfort me. You prepare a table before me in the presence of my enemies. You anoint my head with oil, my cup overflows. Surely, your goodness and love will follow me all the days of my life, and I will dwell in the house of the Lord forever.
- **Psalm 27:14:** Wait for the LORD; be strong and take heart and wait for the LORD.
- **Psalm 50:15:** And call on me in the day of trouble; I will deliver you, and you will honor me.
- **Proverbs 3:5-6:** Trust in the LORD with all your heart and lean not on your own understanding; in all your ways submit to him, and he will make your paths straight.
- **Philippians 4:6**: Do not be anxious about anything, but in every situation, by prayer and petition, with thanksgiving, present your requests to God.

"Bear with each other and forgive one another if any of you has a grievance against someone. Forgive as the Lord forgave you."

Colossians 3:13

CHAPTER 12
THE BETRAYAL OF JEPHTHAH BY HIS BROTHERS

Jephthah's story is found in Judges 11 to 12. He is a Gileadite mighty warrior and a son of a harlot. Because of the manner of his conception, he was driven out from his family by his half-brothers and lived with a gang of worthless men. There came a time when the Israelites were about to fight the Ammonites. The Israelites requested Jephthah to fight for them and Jephthah accepted their request. Jephthah recognized the strength of the Ammonite army. Because of this, he made a vow to God. He said: "And Jephthah made a vow to the Lord, and said, "If You will indeed deliver the people of Ammon into my hands, then it will be that whatever comes out of the doors of my house to meet me, when I return in peace from the people of Ammon, shall surely be the Lord's, and I will offer it up as a burnt offering" (Judges 11:30-31). God granted Jephthah's request and the Israelites won against the Ammonites. Now, it is time for Jephthah to fulfill his vow to God.

When Jephthah arrived home, to his shock, his daughter was the first one who comes out of his house. Obviously, Jephthah did not expect his daughter to meet him. The decision to keep the vow has been very hard for Jephthah since his daughter is his only child. This means that his lineage would not continue anymore. This was a very tragic situation for any Israelite at that time.

Jephthah told his daughter: "And it came to pass, when he saw her, that he tore his clothes, and said, "Alas, my daughter! You have brought me very low! You are among those who trouble me! For I have given my word to the Lord, and I cannot go back on it" (Judges 11:35). As difficult and heartbreaking this has been to Jephthah, he still decided to keep his vow to God.

Lessons to learn from Jephthah's betrayal

- **God can use the circumstances of anyone's betrayal to fulfil his purpose.** Jephthah was a rejected son of a prostitute woman betrayed by his half-brothers. He stepped up to the challenge and became the judge of Israel.

- **Never make promises that you are not able to fulfill**. When you don't keep your word, you lose credibility. "But I say to you that for every idle word man may speak, they will give account of it in the Day of Judgment. For by your words you will be justified, and by your words you will be condemned" (Matthew 12:36-37).

- **Sometimes in life, we may suffer because of the sins of other family members**. Jephthah's mother was a prostitute. This is certainly an act of infidelity on the part of his father. His father sinned and Jephthah came into the world with the fact that he is an illegitimate son. At a very young age, Jephthah must deal with the result of his father's sin.

- **Sometimes, God is more concern about the development of our character than our comfort.** But what will you do if you suffer because of the sin of others? God will not test us beyond our ability to overcome. God allows you to be in a position because He knows that you can bear that trial.

What the Bible says about betrayal

- **Mark 13:12:** And brother will deliver brother over to death, and the father his child, and children will rise against parents and have them put to death.
- **Matthew 24:10:** And then many will fall away and betray one another and hate one another.
- **Matthew 10:21:** Brother will deliver brother over to death, and the father his child, and children will rise against parents and have them put to death.
- **Luke 21:16:** You will be delivered up even by parents and brothers and relatives and friends, and some of you they will put to death.
- **Luke 12:53:** They will be divided, father against son and son against father, mother against daughter and daughter against mother, mother-in-law against her daughter-in-law and daughter-in-law against mother-in-law.
- **Luke 12:51-53:** Do you think that I have come to give peace on earth? No, I tell you, but rather division. For from now on, in one house, there will be five divided, three against two and two against three.

They will be divided, father against son and son against father, mother against daughter and daughter against mother, mother-in-law against her daughter-in-law and daughter-in-law against mother-in-law.

⚔ **Matthew 10:35-36:** For I have come to set a man against his father, and a daughter against her mother, and a daughter-in-law against her mother-in-law. And a person's enemies will be those of his own household.

....

"Bear with each other and forgive one another if any of you has a grievance against someone. Forgive as the Lord forgave you."

Colossians 3:13

....

CHAPTER 13
THE BETRAYAL OF HAGAR AND ISHMAEL

Genesis 18

They returned to Canaan, and a decade passed and still, she and Abraham had no children and so, Sarah offered Hagar, her slavewoman, as a concubine to her husband so that he may have a child. Hagar fell pregnant with Ishmael and, during her pregnancy, Sarah and Hagar's relationship deteriorated rapidly, with Sarah striking her and Hagar fleeing into the desert to avoid her, returning only at the urging of angels. It was then told to Abraham by Yahweh that Sarah would give to him a son, an idea that Sarah, then ninety years old, laughed at, but, as prophesied, she fell pregnant with Isaac and she nursed him herself. She would ultimately demand that Abraham send Hagar and Ishmael away and so, Abraham banished them and sent them into the desert.

Lessons to learn from Hagar's and Ishmael's betrayal

- When you are a man like Abraham and helped to bring a child into the world, it is irrelevant whether the mother of the child was an experiment, a slave, a one-night stand, a wolf in sheep's clothing or a palm reader. It is your godly duty as the father of that child to raise him or her in a godly manner.

- The same human will that caused Abraham to sleep with Hagar is the same that should push him to raise the child that results from that action.
- The Human Will is the most precious but dangerous gift ever given to man.
- Never make your one-minute decision to be more important than the consequences from such a decision.
- The personal actions of blind loyalty can lead to national damage.

What the Bible says about betrayal

- **Mark 13:12:** And brother will deliver brother over to death, and the father his child, and children will rise against parents and have them put to death.
- **Matthew 24:10:** And then many will fall away and betray one another and hate one another.
- **Matthew 10:21:** Brother will deliver brother over to death, and the father his child, and children will rise against parents and have them put to death.
- **Luke 21:16:** You will be delivered up even by parents and brothers and relatives and friends, and some of you they will put to death.
- **Luke 12:53:** They will be divided, father against son and son against father, mother against daughter and daughter against mother, mother-in-law against her daughter-in-law and daughter-in-law against mother-in-law.

⚠ **Luke 12:51-53:** Do you think that I have come to give peace on earth? No, I tell you, but rather division. For from now on in one house there will be five divided, three against two and two against three. They will be divided, father against son and son against father, mother against daughter and daughter against mother, mother-in-law against her daughter-in-law and daughter-in-law against mother-in-law.

⚠ **Matthew 10:35-36:** For I have come to set a man against his father, and a daughter against her mother, and a daughter-in-law against her mother-in-law. And a person's enemies will be those of his own household.

⚠ **2 Timothy 3:1-5:** But mark this: There will be terrible times in the last days. People will be lovers of themselves, lovers of money, boastful, proud, abusive, disobedient to their parents, ungrateful, unholy, without love, unforgiving, slanderous, without self-control, brutal, not lovers of the good, treacherous, rash, conceited, lovers of pleasure rather than lovers of God — having a form of godliness but denying its power. Have nothing to do with such people.

"Bear with each ot her and forgive one another if any of you has a grievance against someone. Forgive as the Lord forgave you."
Colossians 3:13

CHAPTER 14
THE BETRAYAL OF HOSEA BY GOMER

Hosea 1:2-10 NIV

When the Lord began to speak through Hosea, the Lord said to him, "Go, marry a promiscuous woman and have children with her, for like an adulterous wife this land is guilty of unfaithfulness to the Lord." So, he married Gomer, daughter of Diblaim, and she conceived and bore him a son. Then the Lord said to Hosea, "Call him Jezreel, because I will soon punish the house of Jehu for the massacre at Jezreel, and I will put an end to the kingdom of Israel. In that day I will break Israel's bow in the Valley of Jezreel." Gomer conceived again and gave birth to a daughter.

Then the Lord said to Hosea, "Call her Lo-Ruhamah (which means "not loved"), for I will no longer show love to Israel, that I should at all forgive them. Yet, I will show love to Judah; and I will save them — not by bow, sword or battle, or by horses and horsemen, but I, the Lord their God, will save them." After she had weaned Lo-Ruhamah, Gomer had another son. Then the Lord said, "Call him Lo-Ammi (which means "not my people"), for you are not my people, and I am not your God.

"Yet the Israelites will be like the sand on the seashore, which cannot be measured or counted. In the place where it was said to them, 'You are not my people,' they will be called 'children of the living God.'

Gomer's sin and adultery led her into slavery and bondage. While it is unclear whether she literally became a slave, Gomer was indeed enslaved mentally, emotionally, and spiritually to the lifestyle she had chosen. Gomer may have been sold into slavery, but Hosea never forgot her and never stopped loving her, and when God revealed to him that the time was right, Hosea went and redeemed Gomer out of slavery.

Lessons to learn from Hosea's betrayal

- Hosea was a faithful husband; Gomer was an unfaithful wife.
- The prophecy of Hosea is filled with hope because it's not only a story of betrayal, but a story of ransom and renewal.
- Hosea and Gomer's story is the story of God and Israel as well as our story.
- When we, like Gomer, were enslaved, God bought us back.
- When we found ourselves stuck in chains we never intended—chains of insecurity, discontentment or fear—God freed us.
- When we, by our very nature, threw God's love away, He redeemed us.
- The betrayal of Hosea illustrates the spiritual adultery of Israel and God's boundless love for His sinful people.

What the Bible says about betrayal

- **Mark 13:12:** And brother will deliver brother over to death, and the father his child, and children will rise against parents and have them put to death.

- **Matthew 24:10:** And then many will fall away and betray one another and hate one another.

- **Matthew 10:21:** Brother will deliver brother over to death, and the father his child, and children will rise against parents and have them put to death.

- **Luke 21:16:** You will be delivered up even by parents and brothers and relatives and friends, and some of you they will put to death.

- **Luke 12:53:** They will be divided, father against son and son against father, mother against daughter and daughter against mother, mother-in-law against her daughter-in-law and daughter-in-law against mother-in-law.

- **Luke 12:51-53:** Do you think that I have come to give peace on earth? No, I tell you, but rather division. For from now on, in one house, there will be five divided, three against two and two against three. They will be divided, father against son and son against father, mother against daughter and daughter against mother, mother-in-law against her daughter-in-law and daughter-in-law against mother-in-law.

- **Matthew 10:35-36:** For I have come to set a man against his father, and a daughter against her mother, and a daughter-in-law against her mother-in-law. And a person's enemies will be those of his own household.

⚠ **2 Timothy 3:1-5:** But mark this: There will be terrible times in the last days. People will be lovers of themselves, lovers of money, boastful, proud, abusive, disobedient to their parents, ungrateful, unholy, without love, unforgiving, slanderous, without self-control, brutal, not lovers of the good, treacherous, rash, conceited, lovers of pleasure rather than lovers of God-having a form of godliness but denying its power. Have nothing to do with such people.

"Bear with each other and forgive one another if any of you has a grievance against someone. Forgive as the Lord forgave you."

Colossians 3:13

CHAPTER 15
ADULTERY: A SHAMEFUL SECRET BEHIND FAMILY BETRAYALS

Adultery happens when there is consensual sexual intercourse between a married person and a person who is not his or her spouse.

- Betrayal through adultery leaves the innocent spouse with feelings of depression, guilt and humiliation. Self-esteem reaches an all-time low and self-pity reaches an all-time high.

- When a parent commits adultery, it can affect the children in negative ways. A 1989 article published in the *New York Times* states that children may suffer if their parents commit adultery, even if the children are not aware of the affair. The children can sense that the parent is committing mental energy to things outside of the family.

- When a husband or wife commits adultery by seeking self-gratification elsewhere, this action can deeply wound and scar the hearts and minds of their spouse and children.

- Betrayal by adultery comes with a break in trust, fellowship, and intimacy. It is a strong force that uproots a relationship and leaves it hanging and vulnerable.

- When your husband or wife betrays you through adultery, you may decide to forgive and stay together despite, but feel immense loneliness.
- When your husband or wife betrays you through adultery, you might forgive but divorce him or her.
- If the woman or man your spouse cheated with is married, the husband or wife might attempt to bring harm to your family.
- Your husband's or wife's betrayal through adultery with a married woman or man can cause a chain reaction and destroy other marriages and homes.
- Your husband's or wife's betrayal through adultery might result in other consequences like an unwanted child, disease, and the killing of an unborn child through abortion.
- If you are a Christian, your husband's or wife's betrayal through adultery might give others the reason to conclude that all Christians are hypocrites.
- If your marriage survives the adultery and you must start life again, give God the glory and set up strict safeguards to ensure that you are faithful in your marriage commitment. Watch your wandering eyes, guard your thoughts, and avoid any situations that could put your marriage and family in harm's way.
- If your marriage ends up in a divorce after the adultery, give God the glory and start life again with wisdom, knowledge and understanding.

What the Bible says about betrayal

- **Matthew 24:10:** And then many will fall away and betray one another and hate one another.
- **Matthew 10:21:** Brother will deliver brother over to death, and the father his child, and children will rise against parents and have them put to death.
- **Luke 21:16:** You will be delivered up even by parents and brothers and relatives and friends, and some of you they will put to death.
- **Luke 12:53:** They will be divided, father against son and son against father, mother against daughter and daughter against mother, mother-in-law against her daughter-in-law and daughter-in-law against mother-in-law.
- **Luke 12:51-53:** Do you think that I have come to give peace on earth? No, I tell you, but rather division. For from now on, in one house, there will be five divided, three against two and two against three. They will be divided, father against son and son against father, mother against daughter and daughter against mother, mother-in-law against her daughter-in-law and daughter-in-law against mother-in-law.
- **Matthew 10:35-36:** For I have come to set a man against his father, and a daughter against her mother, and a daughter-in-law against her mother-in-law. And a person's enemies will be those of his own household.

"Bear with each other and forgive one another if any of you has a grievance against someone. Forgive as the Lord forgave you."

Colossians 3:13

CHAPTER 16
THE BETRAYAL OF TAMAR BY HER HALF-BROTHER AMNON

Tamar was the beautiful daughter of the great King David and Maacah, a princess from a neighboring kingdom. Her half-brother Amnon became obsessed with her. As a royal princess and a virgin, she was closely watched by a harem of eunuchs. She lived in the women's quarters and could not go outside its walls unless accompanied by other women and guards. There seemed no opportunity for Amnon to be alone with her, much less get her into his bedroom. To make matters worse, she seemed to be intelligent and sexually moral, with only a sisterly interest in him.

Amnon must have discussed his obsession with his clever cousin Jonadab because this young man came up with a plan. They would lure Tamar into Amnon's room on the pretext that her half-brother was ill. He lured her to his room and raped her, then refused to marry her. Their father King David was very angry. She was disgraced and never married. Her embittered brother Absalom rebelled against David but was defeated and killed. Tamar lived out her days in the royal harem.

Lessons to learn from Tamar's betrayal

▲ The most dangerous role of this betrayal was played by the facilitator Jonadab, Amnon's

cousin. The Jonadabs of the family are as guilty as the Amnons, if not more. Without Jonadab's help, Amnon may never have gotten the opportunity to rape Tamar.

- **The rape was not Tamar's fault. She was an innocent victim.** It is very important for a rape victim to hear these words from family, especially from their mother and father. The silence of King David on the matter speaks volumes. Being very angry was not enough. Tamar needed to hear from him that she was not, in any way shape or form, guilty of what happened to her. She needed reassurance from her father, but King David failed her... In fact, he failed his whole family.

- **Sometimes in life, we may suffer because of the sins of other family members** Perhaps King David's own past came back to haunt him. He had raped Bathsheba, even though he knew she was married to Uriah.

- **Hatred will lead to poor decisions with deadly consequences.** But Absalom spoke to Amnon neither good nor bad, for Absalom hated Amnon, because he had violated his sister Tamar. The embittered brother Absalom rebelled against David but was defeated and killed (II Samuel 13:20-22).

- **Unwise counsel is... unwise.** "But Amnon had a friend, whose name was Jonadab, the son of Shimeah, David's brother. And Jonadab was a very crafty man. And he said to him, "O son of the king, why are you so haggard morning after morning? Will you not tell me?" Amnon said to him, "I love Tamar, my brother Absalom's sister." Jonadab said to him, "Lie down on your bed and pretend to be ill. And when your father comes to see you, say to him, 'Let my sister Tamar come and give me bread to eat, and prepare the food in my sight, that I may see it and eat it from her hand." (II Samuel 13:3-5)

What the Bible says about the promises of God

- **Ephesians 5:11:** Take no part in the unfruitful works of darkness, but instead expose them
- **Ephesians 4:29**: Do not let any unwholesome talk come out of your mouths, but only what is helpful for building others up according to their needs, that it may benefit those who listen.
- **1 Corinthians 13:1-13:** Do not be deceived, bad company ruins good morals
- **Matthew 24:10**: And then many will fall away and betray one another and hate one another.
- **Matthew 10:21**: Brother will deliver brother over to death, and the father his child, and children will rise against parents and have them put to death,
- **Luke 21:16:** You will be delivered up even by parents and brothers and relatives and friends, and some of you they will put to death.

- **Luke 12:53**: They will be divided, father against son and son against father, mother against daughter and daughter against mother, mother-in-law against her daughter-in-law and daughter-in-law against mother-in-law."

- **Luke 12:51-52**: Do you think that I have come to give peace on earth? No, I tell you, but rather division. For from now on in one house there will be five divided, three against two and two against three.

- **Matthew 10:35-36:** For I have come to set a man against his father, and a daughter against her mother, and a daughter-in-law against her mother-in-law. And a person's enemies will be those of his own household.

- **Proverbs 12:26**: The righteous choose their friends carefully, but the way of the wicked leads them astray.

- **Proverbs 14:7**: Leave the presence of a fool, for there you do not meet words of knowledge.

"Bear with each other and forgive one another if any of you has a grievance against someone. Forgive as the Lord forgave you."
Colossians 3:13

CHAPTER 17
INCEST: A SHAMEFUL SECRET
BEHIND FAMILY BETRAYALS

Incest can be understood as human sexual activity between family members or close relatives. This typically includes sexual activity between people in consanguinity (blood relations), and sometimes those related by affinity (marriage or stepfamily), adoption, clan, or lineage. Unfortunately, there is no universal law against incest. Laws regarding incest vary considerably between jurisdictions and depend on the type of sexual activity and the nature of the family relationship of the parties involved, as well as the age and sex of the parties.

Incest is a taboo in many cultures. Relationships between cousins may be legal but are frowned upon. Society considers marriage or sexual relations between brothers, sisters, aunts, and uncles as too close. This stance is not just for moral reasons but born of an awareness of the dangers of limiting the gene pool, increasing the likelihood of congenital disabilities and disease in any child borne out of an incestuous union. Today, incest usually occurs accidentally, among individuals who do not know about their close family relationship. History, however, provides us with examples of deliberate incest and shows us a variety of motives behind this socially undesirable practice.

In the past, incest occurred as part of an elite tradition, designed to keep the bloodline of ruling families pure.

However, incest has also manifested as a form of abuse or manipulation. During my 10 years of nursing, I encountered four different women who all claimed that their adopted fathers had sexually molested them at one point or another while they were minors under the care of people, they thought would protect them.

There are also examples of family betrayal by incest from history:

The Case of Virginia Woolf

Virginia was born January 25, 1882 to Julia and Leslie Stephens. Both of her parents had been previously married, and each had children from these earlier relationships. Julia had three other children besides Virginia: Vanessa and their two brothers: George, Stella and Gerald Duckworth. Julia and her new husband were distant parents, which probably explains why they had no idea what was happening with their youngest daughter. Virginia Woolf was assaulted by both of her older half-brothers from when she was only six years old to when she was a young woman. These sexual abuse and betrayal may well have been the root of the mental health problems Virginia suffered for her whole adult life and an intense distaste for sexual contact. She suffered depression from a very early age, as well as anorexia and body dysmorphia.

The Case of Anthony Baekeland

Anthony Baekeland was the son of Bakelite heir Brooks Baekeland and Barbara Daly Baekeland. Born in 1922,

Baekeland was a model whose face graced the pages of *Vogue* and *Harper's Bazaar*. The Baekeland family enjoyed a hedonistic lifestyle of wild parties and infidelity until they eventually took to traveling the world, with Anthony in tow. The boy wanted for nothing materially but was largely ignored by his self-absorbed parents.

Barbara finally became very concerned about her son when she discovered he was gay. Barbara was horrified. She tried to get a young French girl Anthony was friendly with to marry him, but it backfired! Barbara then decided to ply Anthony with prostitutes. When this failed, too, she hatched a plan to "cure" him. Just before they separated, she told her husband: *"You know, I could get Tony over his homosexuality if I just took him to bed."* In 1969, during a holiday in Majorca, she seduced her drunk and high son and had sex with him. This dubious therapy didn't work. Anthony's already uncertain mental health began to decline rapidly. He became paranoid and angry, and doctors diagnosed him with schizophrenia. He began to threaten his mother, brandishing knives at her during arguments. His therapist warned Barbara that her son was going to kill her. She didn't believe him. In 1972, Anthony stabbed his mother to death with a kitchen knife at their London house. He confessed to the murder and was confined to Broadmoor. In 1980, when Anthony was released, he returned home to America, only to attempt to kill Barbara's mother, who he had initially blamed for his mother's death. He later committed suicide in prison.

No matter the variety of motives behind this socially undesirable practice called incest, it remains undeniably true that this practice has and continues to be one of the ultimate and shameful secrets behind many family betrayals. The consequences of incest are damning to both the victim and perpetrator and sometimes, the spectators as well. For the perpetrators and silent spectators of incestuous acts of betrayal, I pray that God's wrath pours upon you in Jesus' name! Amen! For the victims of family betrayal through incest, I pray you don't give up hope. May God who sees all and knows all help you to reap the timely fruits of redemption, forgiveness and healing in Jesus' name, Amen!

What the Bible says about betrayal

- **Ephesians 5:11:** Take no part in the unfruitful works of darkness, but instead expose them.
- **Ephesians 4:29**: Do not let any unwholesome talk come out of your mouths, but only what is helpful for building others up according to their needs, that it may benefit those who listen.
- **1 Corinthians 13:1-13:** Do not be deceived, bad company ruins good morals.
- **Matthew 24:10**: And then many will fall away and betray one another and hate one another.
- **Matthew 10:21**: Brother will deliver brother over to death, and the father his child, and children will rise against parents and have them put to death,
- **Luke 21:16:** You will be delivered up even by parents and brothers and relatives and friends, and some of you they will put to death.

- **Luke 12:53**: They will be divided, father against son and son against father, mother against daughter and daughter against mother, mother-in-law against her daughter-in-law and daughter-in-law against mother-in-law.

- **Luke 12:51-52**: Do you think that I have come to give peace on earth? No, I tell you, but rather division. For from now on, in one house, there will be five divided, three against two and two against three.

- **Matthew 10:35-36:** For I have come to set a man against his father, and a daughter against her mother, and a daughter-in-law against her mother-in-law. And a person's enemies will be those of his own household.

- **Proverbs 12:**26: The righteous choose their friends carefully, but the way of the wicked leads them astray.

- **Proverbs 14:7**: Leave the presence of a fool, for there you do not meet words of knowledge.

"Bear with each other and forgive one another if any of you has a grievance against someone. Forgive as the Lord forgave you."
Colossians 3:13

CHAPTER 18
ADOPTION: A SHAMEFUL SECRET BEHIND FAMILY BETRAYALS

Adoptees often can view their placement into adoption by the birth parents as nothing other than total rejection. For many adoptees, coming to terms with being adopted is a challenging process. Confusion, grief, and self-doubt are common feelings. Even at a young age, they grasp the concept that to be "chosen" means that one was first "un-chosen," reinforcing adoptees' low self-concept. Society promulgates the idea that the "good" adoptee is the one who is reserved and accepts adoption without question. At the other end of the continuum is the "bad" adoptee who is constantly questioning, thereby creating feelings of rejection in the adoptive parents. Most of the betrayal stories in adoption involve betrayal of adopted kids by adopted parents or betrayal of adopted parents by adopted kids. No matter who betrays who, what usually follows the betrayal is abandonment.

What is abandonment?

A loss of love, a feeling of disconnection, being left behind, not belonging, feeling left out, on the outside looking in. It often involves breakup, betrayal, feelings of aloneness and of being different. Often, people experience these feelings singularly, or one after another over a period of months or years, depending on the events in their life. Abandonment and its associated feelings have a personal and individual theme for us all. It is an extremely personal and individual experience. Sometimes, it is lingering grief caused by old losses. Sometimes, it is fear. Sometimes, it is an invisible barrier holding us back from forming relationships or from reaching our true potential. Sometimes, it takes the form of self-sabotage and self-wounding. We can create patterns of abandonment where we self-sabotage ourselves and our relationships.

It also involves biological and chemical processes that underpin our emotional reaction and response to loss. It's hard enough when your biological family lets go of you and even harder when your adoptive parents betray you. On the other hand, it's very difficult when you, as an adoptive parent, open your heart and home to a total stranger, love them the best way you know how, and they stab you in the back.

When betrayal happens, seek God more than ever before. Go to Him for answers and read books and articles by other adoptive parents and adoptees. Find memoirs, essays, blogs, and other publications written about adoption and others who came to terms with their adoption journey. Learning about how other adoptive parents or adoptees cope can help you process your own emotions.

What the Bible says about betrayal

- **Ephesians 5:11:** Take no part in the unfruitful works of darkness, but instead expose them.

- **Ephesians 4:29**: Do not let any unwholesome talk come out of your mouths, but only what is helpful for building others up according to their needs, that it may benefit those who listen.
- **1 Corinthians 13:1-13:** Do not be deceived, bad company ruins good morals.
- **Matthew 24:10**: And then many will fall away and betray one another and hate one another.
- **Matthew 10:21**: Brother will deliver brother over to death, and the father his child, and children will rise against parents and have them put to death.
- **Luke 21:16:** You will be delivered up even by parents and brothers and relatives and friends, and some of you they will put to death.
- **Luke 12:53**: They will be divided, father against son and son against father, mother against daughter and daughter against mother, mother-in-law against her daughter-in-law and daughter-in-law against mother-in-law.
- **Luke 12:51-52**: Do you think that I have come to give peace on earth? No, I tell you, but rather division. For from now on, in one house, there will be five divided, three against two and two against three.
- **Matthew 10:35-36:** For I have come to set a man against his father, and a daughter against her mother, and a daughter-in-law against her mother-in-law. And a person's enemies will be those of his own household.
- **Proverbs 12:**26: The righteous choose their friends carefully, but the way of the wicked leads them astray.

⚠ **Proverbs 14:7**: Leave the presence of a fool, for there you do not meet words of knowledge.

....

"Bear with each other and forgive one another if any of you has a grievance against someone. Forgive as the Lord forgave you."

Colossians 3:13

....

CHAPTER 19
WHEN YOUR CHILD RIPS YOUR HEART INTO A MILLION LITTLE PIECES

The wisdom of God warns parents to start children off on the way they should go, and even when they are old, they will not turn from it **(Proverbs 22:6)**. God's wisdom also calls on children to honor their father and mother, so that they may live long in the land the LORD God is giving them **(Exodus 20:12)**.

In general, when the right and godly foundation is laid for the child, they grow up to be responsible, respectful loyal and God-fearing members of the family and community. Sometimes, life happens and no matter how solid the foundation, the child departs from the good upbringing and becomes a thorn in the family flesh by dishonoring one or both parents. Other times, life happens to a child with a shaky foundation, but they build a foundation for themselves as adults and become God-fearing, loving, loyal, dedicated members of the family. In any of these cases, give thanks to God.

What the Bible says about betrayal

- **Mark 13:12:** And brother will deliver brother over to death, and the father his child, and children will rise against parents and have them put to death.

⬥ **Matthew 24:10:** And then many will fall away and betray one another and hate one another.

⬥ **Matthew 10:21:** Brother will deliver brother over to death, and the father his child, and children will rise against parents and have them put to death.

⬥ **Luke 21:16:** You will be delivered up even by parents and brothers and relatives and friends, and some of you they will put to death.

⬥ **Luke 12:53:** They will be divided, father against son and son against father, mother against daughter and daughter against mother, mother-in-law against her daughter-in-law and daughter-in-law against mother-in-law."

⬥ **Luke 12:51-52:** Do you think that I have come to give peace on earth? No, I tell you, but rather division. For from now on, in one house, there will be five divided, three against two and two against three.

⬥ **Matthew 10:35-36:** For I have come to set a man against his father, and a daughter against her mother, and a daughter-in-law against her mother-in-law. And a person's enemies will be those of his own household.

⬥ **Proverbs 22:6:** Start children off on the way they should go, and even when they are old, they will not turn from it.

⬥ **Proverbs 12:22:** Anxiety weighs down the heart, but a kind word cheers it up.

⬥ **2 Timothy 3:1-5:** But mark this: There will be terrible times in the last days. People will be lovers of themselves, lovers of money, boastful, proud, abusive, disobedient to their parents, ungrateful, unholy, without love, unforgiving, slanderous, without self-control, brutal, not lovers of the good, treacherous, rash, conceited, lovers of pleasure rather than lovers of God—having a form of godliness but denying its power. Have nothing to do with such people.

▲ **Psalm 9:9:** The Lord is a refuge for the oppressed, a stronghold in times of trouble.

"Bear with each other and forgive one another if any of you has a grievance against someone. Forgive as the Lord forgave you."

Colossians 3:13

CHAPTER 20
WHEN YOUR PARENT RIPS YOUR HEART INTO A MILLION LITTLE PIECES

God's wisdom warns parents not to provoke their children to anger but to bring them up in the discipline and instruction of the Lord **(Ephesians 4:6)**. When parents fail to do this and end up betraying their children and ripping their hearts into a million little pieces, the consequences can be life-altering to both the parents and the betrayed child.

The wisdom of God warns parents not to provoke their children in a way that ends up discouraging them **(Colossians 3:21-22)**. Fathers, do not provoke your children to anger; instead, bring them up in the discipline and instruction of the Lord **(Ephesians 4:6)**.

God exhorts children to their honor father and mother. He values honoring parents enough to include it in the Ten Commandments **(Exodus 20:12)** and again in the New Testament: "Children, obey your parents in the Lord, for this is right. Honor your father and mother which is the first commandment with a promise, so that it may be well with you, and that you may live long on the earth" **(Ephesians 6:1-3)**. Honoring parents is the only command in Scripture that promises long life as a reward.

What the Bible says about betrayal

- **Mark 13:12:** And brother will deliver brother over to death, and the father his child, and children will rise against parents and have them put to death.

- **Matthew 24:10:** And then many will fall away and betray one another and hate one another.

- **Matthew 10:21:** Brother will deliver brother over to death, and the father his child, and children will rise against parents and have them put to death.

- **Luke 21:16:** You will be delivered up even by parents and brothers and relatives and friends, and some of you they will put to death.

- **Luke 12:53:** They will be divided, father against son and son against father, mother against daughter and daughter against mother, mother-in-law against her daughter-in-law and daughter-in-law against mother-in-law.

- **Luke 12:51-52:** Do you think that I have come to give peace on earth? No, I tell you, but rather division. For from now on, in one house, there will be five divided, three against two and two against three.

- **Matthew 10:35-36:** For I have come to set a man against his father, and a daughter against her mother, and a daughter-in-law against her mother-in-law. And a person's enemies will be those of his own household.

- **2 Timothy 3:1-5:** But mark this: There will be terrible times in the last days. People will be lovers of themselves, lovers of money, boastful, proud, abusive, disobedient to their parents, ungrateful, unholy, without love, unforgiving, slanderous, without self-control, brutal, not lovers of the good, treacherous, rash, conceited, lovers of pleasure rather than lovers of God, having a form of godliness but denying its power. Have nothing to do with such people.

- **Psalm 9:9:** The Lord is a refuge for the oppressed, a stronghold in times of trouble.

"Bear with each other and forgive one another if any of you has a grievance against someone. Forgive as the Lord forgave you."

Colossians 3:13

CHAPTER 21
WHEN A SPOUSE RIPS YOUR HEART INTO A MILLION LITTLE PIECES

Marriage is between one man and one woman. Here is what Jesus said when He was questioned about marriage and divorce in Matthew 19:4-6:

> *"And He answered and said, "Haven't you read," he replied, "that at the beginning the Creator 'made them male and female,' and said, 'For this reason a man will leave his father and mother and be united to his wife, and the two will become one flesh'? So, they are no longer two, but one flesh. Therefore, what God has joined, let no one separate."*

The ultimate shameful secret of spousal betrayal happens when marriage that is supposed to be two people becoming one gets so crowded that a census is required to determine who is who in the marriage circus! Spousal betrayal comes like a wolf in sheep's clothing. It is hard enough to trust one person, let alone a whole village of wolves in sheep's clothing! When your spouse betrays you and rips your heart into a million little pieces, thank God and give God the glory. When you've been cheated on, the first thing to decide is whether to go through the grueling and often painful process of putting your relationship back on track. When a spouse betrays you and rips your heart into a million little pieces, pick up the pieces and brace yourself. Nevertheless, give God the glory. It could have been worse, and it can get better. Keep hope alive and keep trusting God!

How to overcome spousal betrayal

- Pray to God, forgive the cheating spouse by handing him or her over to God almighty.
- Don't betray the spouse who betrayed you. Common sense dictates that two wrongs don't make a right. If your spouse cheats on you, the ultimate shameful thing is to cheat on him or her as well.
- Take time away to experience solitude and carefully reflect on the spousal betrayal, the marriage relationship, and other aspects of your life.
- When your voice of reason returns, speak to your spouse who betrayed you.
- Talk to a professional third party before you consider options like divorce or manslaughter. (Manslaughter should never be an option when a spouse betrays you, God forbid!)
- It's the job of the cheater or the betrayer to make a partner feel safe again, not the other way around. If the betrayed partner wants to know everything about the affair, that, too, needs to be negotiated to try to restore the terrible breach of trust.
- Redefine the relationship, find out what is missing, and set your marriage expectation and responsibility clock back to a better time.

- It takes time for trust to be reestablished, so work through your marriage issues with the recognition that things won't get better overnight.
- If you pray and believe the best solution to your betrayal is divorce, give God the glory and ride on.

What the Bible says about betrayal

- **Mark 13:12:** And brother will deliver brother over to death, and the father his child, and children will rise against parents and have them put to death.
- **Matthew 24:10:** And then many will fall away and betray one another and hate one another.
- **Matthew 10:21:** Brother will deliver brother over to death, and the father his child, and children will rise against parents and have them put to death,
- **Luke 21:16:** You will be delivered up even by parents and brothers and relatives and friends, and some of you they will put to death.
- **Luke 12:53:** They will be divided, father against son and son against father, mother against daughter and daughter against mother, mother-in-law against her daughter-in-law and daughter-in-law against mother-in-law.
- **Luke 12:51-52:** Do you think that I have come to give peace on earth? No, I tell you, but rather division. For from now on, in one house, there will be five divided, three against two and two against three.

- **Matthew 10:35-36:** For I have come to set a man against his father, and a daughter against her mother, and a daughter-in-law against her mother-in-law. And a person's enemies will be those of his own household.
- **Psalm 9:9:** The Lord is a refuge for the oppressed, a stronghold in times of trouble.
- **2 Timothy 3:1-5:** But mark this: There will be terrible times in the last days. People will be lovers of themselves, lovers of money, boastful, proud, abusive, disobedient to their parents, ungrateful, unholy, without love, unforgiving, slanderous, without self-control, brutal, not lovers of the good, treacherous, rash, conceited, lovers of pleasure rather than lovers of God—having a form of godliness but denying its power. Have nothing to do with such people.

"Bear with each other and forgive one another if any of you has a grievance against someone. Forgive as the Lord forgave you."
Colossians 3:13

CHAPTER 22
WHEN A SIBLING RIPS YOUR HEART INTO A MILLION LITTLE PIECES

If you accept rubbish from family long enough, you will soon become the dumping ground for family shit. Just because you share the same DNA with a sibling, doesn't mean you share the same values. Just because you are the oldest sibling, it doesn't mean you are the wisest. Just because you are the youngest sibling, it doesn't make you the dumbest. Just because you are the richest sibling, it doesn't earn you the right to be arrogant. Just because you are the most respected sibling, it doesn't mean you should be the most abusive. Just because you are the youngest sibling, it doesn't make you a permanent footstool for the older siblings to rest their tired and angry feet.

The adage "Wisdom comes with age" is for those who diligently seek wisdom as they age. If you kick a sleeping dog hard enough, it will bite you. When God sets a table for you in front of your enemies, it makes sense that some of those enemies will be from your family **(Psalm 23)**. Don't be naive to think everyone in your family will celebrate your success the way you think they should. Your success may sometimes be yours and yours alone to celebrate. When a sibling rips your heart into a million little pieces, please don't waste your precious time recruiting other family members to join you walk away from him or her. If you are hurt enough, you don't need help walking or running away from that toxic family member. Blind loyalty, even to family, is foolishness and a disaster waiting to happen, so watch out for the Cains in your family. Family means love, support, kindness, nurturing, and struggle. When hate, envy, lack of empathy and viciousness show up, run for your sanity and destiny.

What the Bible says about betrayal

- **Mark 13:12:** And brother will deliver brother over to death, and the father his child, and children will rise against parents and have them put to death.
- **Matthew 24:10:** And then many will fall away and betray one another and hate one another.
- **Matthew 10:21**: Brother will deliver brother over to death, and the father his child, and children will rise against parents and have them put to death.
- **Luke 21:16:** You will be delivered up even by parents and brothers and relatives and friends, and some of you they will put to death.
- **Luke 12:53:** They will be divided, father against son and son against father, mother against daughter and daughter against mother, mother-in-law against her daughter-in-law and daughter-in-law against mother-in-law.
- **Luke 12:51-52**: Do you think that I have come to give peace on earth? No, I tell you, but rather division. For from now on, in one house, there will be five divided, three against two and two against three.

▲ **Matthew 10:35-36**: For I have come to set a man against his father, and a daughter against her mother, and a daughter-in-law against her mother-in-law. And a person's enemies will be those of his own household.

▲ **Psalm 9:9:** The Lord is a refuge for the oppressed, a stronghold in times of trouble.

▲ **2 Timothy 3:1-5**: But mark this: There will be terrible times in the last days. People will be lovers of themselves, lovers of money, boastful, proud, abusive, disobedient to their parents, ungrateful, unholy, without love, unforgiving, slanderous, without self-control, brutal, not lovers of the good, treacherous, rash, conceited, lovers of pleasure rather than lovers of God-having a form of godliness but denying its power. Have nothing to do with such people.

"Bear with each other and forgive one another if any of you has a grievance against someone. Forgive as the Lord forgave you."
Colossians 3:13

CHAPTER 23
WHEN RELATIVES RIP YOUR HEART INTO A MILLION LITTLE PIECES

We all know how in the family, you can sometimes be closer to grandparents than to your own parents, closer to your nieces and nephews and love them unconditionally. Sometimes, your aunts and uncles are so special to you that you simply cherish them. And if you are from an African culture like me, there is no such thing as extended family. Family is family!

If all your relationships are going well, give God the glory. If some are rocky, give God the glory. Betrayal from the family is the ultimate wound that really stinks. Relationships in the family can be complex, but if these relationships are based on unconditional love and mutual respect, they can hopefully be better managed. Depending on your individual relationships in the family, betrayal from a niece or a nephew once removed can hurt even more than betrayal from your own sibling, child or spouse.

What the Bible says about betrayal

- **Deuteronomy 31:6:** Be strong and courageous. Do not be afraid or terrified because of them, for the LORD your God goes with you; He will never leave you nor forsake you.

- **Mark 13:12:** And brother will deliver brother over to death, and the father his child, and children will rise against parents and have them put to death.
- **Matthew 24:10**: And then many will fall away and betray one another and hate one another.
- **Matthew 10:21**: Brother will deliver brother over to death, and the father his child, and children will rise against parents and have them put to death.
- **Luke 21:16:** You will be delivered up even by parents and brothers and relatives and friends, and some of you they will put to death.
- **Luke 12:53**: They will be divided, father against son and son against father, mother against daughter and daughter against mother, mother-in-law against her daughter-in-law and daughter-in-law against mother-in-law.
- **Luke 12:51-53:** Do you think that I have come to give peace on earth? No, I tell you, but rather division. For from now on in one house there will be five divided, three against two and two against three. They will be divided, father against son and son against father, mother against daughter and daughter against mother, mother-in-law against her daughter-in-law and daughter-in-law against mother-in-law.
- **Matthew 10:35-36**: For I have come to set a man against his father, and a daughter against her mother, and a daughter-in-law against her mother-in-law. And a person's enemies will be those of his own household.

- **Psalm 9:9:** The Lord is a refuge for the oppressed, a stronghold in times of trouble.
- **2 Timothy 3:1-5**: But mark this: There will be terrible times in the last days. People will be lovers of themselves, lovers of money, boastful, proud, abusive, disobedient to their parents, ungrateful, unholy, without love, unforgiving, slanderous, without self-control, brutal, not lovers of the good, treacherous, rash, conceited, lovers of pleasure rather than lovers of Godhaving a form of godliness but denying its power. Have nothing to do with such people.

"Bear with each other and forgive one another if any of you has a grievance against someone. Forgive as the Lord forgave you."

Colossians 3:13

CHAPTER 24
COMMUNICATION TECHNOLOGY: A MEDIUM OF FAMILY BETRAYALS

Please do not let family use communication technology to rip your heart into a million pieces more than once. When they take you unawares the first time, block them and help send them back to the age of reason, when there were no phones and other forms of communication technology.

Growing up in an African village, when you were mad at somebody, you either walked up to them or to their house to confront them or you sent a child with a message to that family member. In the case of a child sent on such an errand, most of the time, they will forget some or the whole message by the time they got to that family member and all they will probably say is "Mama said I should come check on you." By the time all is said and done between the errand boy giving the wrong message and the family member beating them up, the voice of reason will tell them it is not the right thing to say what you wanted to say. God has intervened, and the damage has been controlled most of the time.

In the event where the angry family member decides to go confront the other family member herself or himself, the voice of reason will sometimes reappear before they even get to that family member. Communication technology came with the good, the bad, and the ugly. Use it with wisdom and understanding. Always think before you press

SEND! What is sent can hardly be unsent. Think, think, and think before you post, send, tweet, or deliver any piece of information to a loved one or anybody.

What to always remember about communication technology

- Communication technology will dull your sense of reason if you let it.
- Communication technology cannot and will never replace God.
- There are things only God knows, understands, and can do.
- Communication technology improves communication.
- Communication technology cuts through cultural barriers.
- Communication technology is fast, and not safe.
- It is no surprise that the fast-paced consumption of digital media has resulted in a shorter average attention span.
- More technology means less creative thinking.
- When words run short, emojis help you exaggerate how you really feel.

What the Bible says about betrayal

- **Deuteronomy 31:6:** Be strong and courageous. Do not be afraid or terrified because of them, for the LORD your God goes with you; he will never leave you nor forsake you.

⚔ **Mark 13:12:** And brother will deliver brother over to death, and the father his child, and children will rise against parents and have them put to death.

⚔ **Matthew 24:10**: And then many will fall away and betray one another and hate one another.

⚔ **Matthew 10:21**: Brother will deliver brother over to death, and the father his child, and children will rise against parents and have them put to death.

⚔ **Luke 21:16:** You will be delivered up even by parents and brothers and relatives and friends, and some of you they will put to death.

⚔ **Luke 12:53**: They will be divided, father against son and son against father, mother against daughter and daughter against mother, mother-in-law against her daughter-in-law and daughter-in-law against mother-in-law.

⚔ **Luke 12:51-53:** Do you think that I have come to give peace on earth? No, I tell you, but rather division. For from now on, in one house, there will be five divided, three against two and two against three. They will be divided, father against son and son against father, mother against daughter and daughter against mother, mother-in-law against her daughter-in-law and daughter-in-law against mother-in-law.

⚔ **Matthew 10:35-36**: For I have come to set a man against his father, and a daughter against her mother, and a daughter-in-law against her mother-in-law. And a person's enemies will be those of his own household.

- **Psalm 9:9:** The Lord is a refuge for the oppressed, a stronghold in times of trouble.
- **2 Timothy 3:1-5**: But mark this: There will be terrible times in the last days. People will be lovers of themselves, lovers of money, boastful, proud, abusive, disobedient to their parents, ungrateful, unholy, without love, unforgiving, slanderous, without self-control, brutal, not lovers of the good, treacherous, rash, conceited, lovers of pleasure rather than lovers of God—having a form of godliness but denying its power. Have nothing to do with such people.

....

"Bear with each other and forgive one another if any of you has a grievance against someone. Forgive as the Lord forgave you."

Colossians 3:13

....

CHAPTER 25
EMOTIONAL AND DIVINE INTELLIGENCE WHEN DEALING WITH THE "CAINS" IN YOUR FAMILY

Before you go nuts on that family member who used a phone call, text message, Messenger, WhatsApp, Twitter and Instagram to rip your heart into a million pieces, consider the following:

1. You are defined by what comes out of your mouth, so watch your words!
2. The power of life and death lies in the tongue, so guard your tongue!
3. Be sure to taste your words before you spit them out, so watch your words!
4. The tongue may be soft, but it can break bones, so watch your words!
5. Even a fool can pass for a wise man if he knows when to shut his mouth.
6. Words are free but don't use them foolishly, so watch your words!
7. Your future is more important than your past, so watch your tongue!

8. Never make a permanent decision regarding a temporal problem, so watch your words!

9. Your successful future has already been guaranteed by God. But it's your choice to get there, so watch your words and your actions.

10. Your future is not ahead of you, but trapped within you, so protect it with your tongue.

11. It's always best to be on a higher moral ground than your opponent, so watch your words.

12. Wisdom is situational. An eye for an eye is not the best thing to do most of the time. Think and think again before you act!

Lack of respect in the family can sometimes be the ultimate and shameful secret of many family betrayals. Respect is the core of family relationships and harmony. A family is constantly changing and growing, if not in numbers, then in life experiences. Respect can be given in each new situation to establish and continue a pattern of respect among the family members. Respect, like charity, must begin at home. Respect yourself and those around you, and then extend it to strangers outside the family.

What the Bible says about the power of the tongue

- **Colossians 4:6:** Let your conversation be always full of grace, seasoned with salt, so that you may know how to answer everyone.

- **Ephesians 4:29:** Do not let any unwholesome talk come out of your mouths, but only what is helpful for building others up according to their needs, that it may benefit those who listen.
- **James 3:5:** Likewise, the tongue is a small part of the body, but it makes great boasts. Consider what a great forest is set on fire by a small spark.
- **Matthew 15:10-11:** Jesus called the crowd to Him and said, "Listen and understand. What goes into someone's mouth does not defile them, but what comes out of their mouth, that is what defiles them."
- **Matthew 15:18:** But the things that come out of a person's mouth come from the heart, and these defile them.
- **Proverbs 10:19:** Sin is not ended by multiplying words, but the prudent hold their tongues.
- **Proverbs 15:4:** The soothing tongue is a tree of life, but a perverse tongue crushes the spirit.
- **Proverbs 15:28:** The heart of the righteous weighs its answers, but the mouth of the wicked gushes evil.
- **Proverbs 13:3:** Those who guard their lips preserve their lives, but those who speak rashly will come to ruin.
- **Proverbs 18:20-21:** From the fruit of their mouth a person's stomach is filled; with the harvest of their lips they are satisfied. The tongue has the power of life and death, and those who love it will eat its fruit.
- **Proverbs 21:23:** Those who guard their mouths and their tongues keep themselves from calamity.

- **Proverbs 31:26:** She speaks with wisdom, and faithful instruction is on her tongue.
- **1 Peter 3:10:** Whoever would love life and see good days must keep their tongue from evil and their lips from deceitful speech.
- **Psalm 34:13:** Keep your tongue from evil and your lips from telling lies.
- **Proverbs 23:9:** Do not speak to fools, for they will scorn your prudent words.

"Bear with each other and forgive one another if any of you has a grievance against someone. Forgive as the Lord forgave you."

Colossians 3:13

CHAPTER 26
MENTAL ILLNESS: A SECRET BEHIND FAMILY BETRAYALS

Mental illness is an illness that affects the way people think, feel, behave, or interact with others. It can be that hidden secret behind family betrayal. A family member's disloyalty, bad faith, or deception might be triggered by mental illness. A family member's violence, mood swings, lack of interest, anxiety may be due to an underlying mental illness. Some of the main groups of mental disorders are:

- mood disorders (such as depression or bipolar disorder)
- anxiety disorders
- personality disorders
- psychotic disorders (such as schizophrenia)
- eating disorders
- trauma-related disorders (such as post-traumatic stress disorder)

What the Bible Says about mental illness

It is important to note that the Bible never explicitly speaks about mental illness in terms of how we would define it in modern times. However, it provides insight on how we should view and respond to those who are battling with their own minds.

Our earthly lives are limited and eventually, our bodies will fail us. This also applies to our minds. Throughout Scripture, we see biblical figures such as David (Psalm 38:4), Job (Job 3:26), Elijah (1 Kings 19:4), and Jonah (Jonah 4:3) dealing with deep feelings of despair, anger, depression, and loneliness. While some of these things can be attributed to spiritual warfare, they can also be of a physical nature. We also see characters where their mental state is somehow connected to their spiritual state (Daniel 4:28-33; 1 Samuel 16:14). Since we know that our bodies are prone to go awry at times, it's possible that what we are experiencing is related to chemical imbalances or other things happening within our brains.

Always remember that taking medication amid mental illness doesn't show a lack of faith in the ability of the Lord to sustain us through the suffering. Rather, it may allow some to experience God with more clarity. The hope we have during mental suffering is that the Lord knows, hears, heals, and is always ready to forgive our sins when we come to Him (1 John 1:9). If He did it for David, Job, Elijah and Jonah, He can do it for us as well. Remain prayerful and hopeful.

God is close to those who are suffering. What is constant throughout Scripture is that God provides comfort to the suffering and meets the needs of the brokenhearted (Psalm 34:18, Psalm 145:18). His Word promises that everything is working together for the good of those who love Him and are called according to His purpose (Romans 8:28). It is outside of God's character to senselessly torment those He loves (Lamentations 3:31-33). We know that the trials that we are experiencing on this earth, while difficult and uncomfortable, are for the testing of our faith (James 1:2), to produce endurance and character (Romans 5:3-5) and are never without purpose.

Most of us are not mental health experts, so we should avoid diagnosing and stigmatizing family members who are acting strange. When we encounter family members who suffer from mental illness, we should be hesitant to provide our opinion on what caused it or how it should be solved. Encourage them to seek professional and medical help, if need be. Be available. Walk with them, shouldering one another's burdens in order to fulfill the law of Christ (Galatians 6:2).

What the Bible says about the promises of God

- **Deuteronomy 31:6:** Be strong and courageous. Do not be afraid or terrified because of them, for the LORD your God goes with you; He will never leave you nor forsake you.

- **Ephesians 3:20:** Now to him who can do immeasurably more than all we ask or imagine, according to His power that is at work within us.

- **Hebrews 7:25:** Therefore, He can save completely those who come to God through Him because He always lives to intercede for them.

- **Isaiah 41:10:** So, do not fear, for I am with you; do not be dismayed, for I am your God. I will strengthen you and help you; I will uphold you with My righteous right hand.

- **Psalm 23:4-6**: Even though I walk through the darkest valley, I will fear no evil, for You are with me; Your rod and Your staff, they comfort me. You prepare a table before me in the presence of my enemies. You anoint my head with oil, my cup overflows. Surely, your goodness and love will follow me all the days of my life, and I will dwell in the house of the Lord forever.
- **Psalm 27:14:** Wait for the LORD; be strong and take heart and wait for the LORD.
- **Psalm 50:15:** Call on me in the day of trouble; I will deliver you, and you will honor Me.
- **Proverbs 3:5-6:** Trust in the LORD with all your heart and lean not on your own understanding; in all your ways submit to Him, and He will make your paths straight.
- **Philippians 4:6**: Do not be anxious about anything, but in every situation, by prayer and petition, with thanksgiving, present your requests to God.

....

"Bear with each other and forgive one another if any of you has a grievance against someone. Forgive as the Lord forgave you."

Colossians 3:13

....

CHAPTER 27
IGNORANCE: A SHAMEFUL SECRET BEHIND FAMILY BETRAYALS

Ignorance is a lack of knowledge and information. The word "ignorant" is an adjective that describes a person in the state of being unaware and can describe individuals who deliberately disregard important information or facts, or individuals who are unaware of important information or facts.

As my Luminary Papa Asafor put it, "If you think education is expensive, try ignorance."

Start by knowing yourself:

1. Knowing oneself is the beginning of all wisdom (Aristotle). Having wisdom will open so many things for you.
2. Knowing who you are can facilitate the learning and knowledge about other family members.
3. Knowing who you are can help you realize who God created you to be.
4. Knowing who you are is a secure foundation to developing other relationships.
5. The relationship with yourself is the most important relationship, second only to your relationship with

God. If you cherish and nurture this relationship, life has a way of leading you to more joy, prosperity and satisfaction.

That said, I will not hesitate to mention here that the ignorant can play a significant role in family betrayals. There may be people in your family that lack knowledge and information about certain aspects of you and your life. It is even more frustrating when the people you love the most in the family deliberately ignore or disregard important information or facts about who you really are and what you stand for. It is difficult to protect that which you don't know or don't want to know.

Sometimes in the family setting, the family members that lack integrity are the ones that are quick to judge those with integrity and question their values. Integrity is the quality of being honest and having strong moral principles (morally upright). The phrase "Ignorance is bliss" was coined by Thomas Gray in his *Ode on a Distant Prospect of Eton College*. It means if you do not know about something, you do not worry about it. Unfortunately, that does not apply to family relationships.

In order to love unconditionally, you must seek to know unconditionally. Knowing your family member is not an option, but an obligation in family relationships. Have you ever wondered why some friends are more important to you and your happiness than some close family members? Friendship is about knowing, accepting, and respecting each other. Family relationships are supposed to be an advanced and more intimate friendship. But the reality is that often, we take family for granted, thinking we already know them and ending up hurting them or being hurt due to our lack of knowledge. People often like to remain ignorant because it's easy or they simply don't have the capacity to see beyond themselves or the situation.

Ignorance of the law is no excuse at all; so is ignorance about each other in the family. So, spouses, try to know and respect each other. Parents, do learn about your children to know and respect them. Children, ask your parents questions, observe them, try to know and respect them. Siblings, consciously learn, know and respect each other. Adoptive parents, please make extra effort to learn and know your adopted child or children. Adopted children, I know you have a lot on your mind, but please make extra effort to learn and know your adoptive parents and the rest of the family. Knowing each other can help limit or mitigate family betrayals.

What the Bible says about ignorance

- **Ephesians 4:18**: They are darkened in their understanding, alienated from the life of God because of the ignorance that is in them, due to their hardness of heart.
- **Romans 1:19-20**: For what can be known about God is plain to them, because God has shown it to them. For His invisible attributes, namely, His eternal power and divine nature, have been clearly perceived, ever since the creation of the world, in the things that have been made. So, they are without excuse.
- **Hosea 4:6**: My people are destroyed for lack of knowledge; because you have rejected knowledge, I

reject you from being a priest to me. And since you have forgotten the law of your God, I also will forget your children.

⚜ **Acts 17:30-31:** The times of ignorance God overlooked, but now He commands all people everywhere to repent because He has fixed a day on which He will judge the world in righteousness by a man whom He has appointed; and of this He has given assurance to all by raising him from the dead.

⚜ **Proverbs 19:2:** Desire without knowledge is not good, and whoever makes haste with his feet misses his way.

⚜ **Hebrews 5:2**: Says that Jesus is "able to deal gently with those who are ignorant and are going astray since he himself is subject to weakness." God has great patience, even with the ignorant. Even when we are willfully ignorant, He gives us a multitude of opportunities to learn (2 Peter 3:9). Paul said that God showed him mercy because, before Jesus saved him, he had "acted in ignorance and unbelief" (1 Timothy 1:13: Acts 3:17).

....

"Bear with each other and forgive one another if any of you has a grievance against someone. Forgive as the Lord forgave you."

Colossians 3:13

....

CHAPTER 28
SUBSTANCE ABUSE AND ADDICTION: SECRETS BEHIND FAMILY BETRAYALS

Addiction is a chronic disease that has the potential to negatively affect a person's life and health as well as the life and health of their loved ones. One of the casualties of a battle with addiction is the trail of damaged relationships it leaves in its wake.

When one person in the family develops a substance abuse issue, it doesn't solely affect them. No matter what their drug of choice happens to be, their addiction is a family disease, since it causes stress to the people living in the family home and to those people closest to the addict.

Without a doubt, substance abuse and addiction are two of the ultimate shameful secrets behind some family betrayals. They have the potential to interfere with normal family life, routines and emotional energy. A person living with an addiction may behave in an erratic manner, depending on whether they are sober, drunk or high, or in recovery. Unfortunately, it can take time for a family to realize that they are dealing with a loved one who has developed an addiction to drugs or alcohol.

The early stages of the disease can be subtle. Addicts can be very good at persuading family members that an episode where they were under the influence was an isolated one and that it will never happen again. Unfortunately, in the case of someone who is living with an addiction, it always happens again. Most of the time, addicts thrive in confusion and disagreement in the family. The addict realizes that if the family is in turmoil, they'll be able to feed their addiction relatively undisturbed. They are not going to allow anything to get in the way of feeding the addiction. The victims of substance abuse and addiction are usually spouses, children, parents, and friends.

Negative effects of substance abuse and addiction on the family

1. Peaceful, loving homes can be divided by the strain caused by substance abuse and addiction.
2. Spouses, children, and parents who witness a family member struggling with addiction experience emotional damage, as well as financial, legal, medical, and other consequences.
3. Domestic violence is an abusive pattern often coupled with the impulsive effects of substance abuse and addiction.
4. There is a great deal of evidence showing a close link between sexual violence and substance abuse (Resnick, Acierno, & Kilpatrick, 1997).

About 21.5 million Americans have a substance abuse disorder, according to the American Society of Addiction Medicine. This figure applies to people aged 12 and older. Of this number, about 1.9 million people developed an addiction to prescription pain medicines and 586,000 had an addiction to heroin. If your family member is struggling with substance abuse and addiction, don't give up. Seek God through prayers and professional help. With the right kind of help, repairing relationships after addiction is possible in Jesus' name. Professional help is needed for people struggling with drug addiction to learn how to live a sober lifestyle and learn how to live without their drug of choice.

What the Bible says about substance abuse and addiction

- **1 Corinthians 10:13: Top of Form** No temptation has overtaken you that is not common to man. God is faithful, and He will not let you be tempted beyond your ability, but with the temptation, He will also provide the way of escape, that you may be able to endure it.
- **1 Corinthians 15:33 ESV:** Do not be deceived: "Bad company ruins good morals."
- **1 Corinthians 6:19-20 ESV**: Or do you not know that your body is a temple of the Holy Spirit within you, whom you have from God? You are not your own, for you were bought with a price. So, glorify God in your body.
- **Galatians 5:19-21 ESV**: Now the works of the flesh are evident: sexual immorality, impurity, sensuality, idolatry, sorcery, enmity, strife, jealousy, fits of anger, rivalries, dissensions, divisions, envy, drunkenness, orgies, and things like these. I warn you, as I warned you

before, that those who do such things will not inherit the kingdom of God.

▲ **Philippians 4:13 ESV:** I can do all things through Him who strengthens me.

▲ **1 Corinthians 6:12 ESV:** All things are lawful for me," but not all things are helpful. "All things are lawful for me," but I will not be enslaved by anything.

▲ **Matthew 6:13 ESV:** And lead us not into temptation but deliver us from evil.

▲ **Proverbs 20:1 ESV:** Wine is a mocker, strong drink a brawler, and whoever is led astray by it is not wise.

▲ **1 Peter 5:8 (NIV):** Be alert and of sober mind. Your enemy the devil prowls around like a roaring lion looking for someone to devour.

▲ **1 Corinthians 6:9-11 ESV:** Or do you not know that the unrighteous will not inherit the kingdom of God? Do not be deceived: neither the sexually immoral, nor idolaters, nor adulterers, nor men who practice homosexuality, nor thieves, nor the greedy, nor drunkards, nor revilers, nor swindlers will inherit the kingdom of God. And such were some of you. But you were washed, you were sanctified, you were justified in the name of the Lord Jesus Christ and by the Spirit of our God.

▲ **Matthew 5:13-16 ESV:** You are the salt of the earth, but if salt has lost its taste, how shall its saltiness be restored? It is no longer good for anything except to be thrown out and trampled under people's feet. You are the light of the world. A city set on a hill cannot be hidden. Nor do people light a lamp and put it under a basket, but on a stand, and it gives light to all in the house. In the same way, let your light shine before others, so that they may see your good works and give glory to your Father who is in heaven.

⋏ **Isaiah 5:11 ESV:** Woe to those who rise early in the morning, that they may run after strong drink, who tarry late into the evening as wine inflames them!

⋏ **Psalm 69:1-36 ESV:** To the choirmaster: according to lilies of David. Save me, O God! For the waters have come up to my neck. I sink in deep mire, where there is no foothold; I have come into deep waters, and the flood sweeps over me. I am weary with my crying out; my throat is parched. My eyes grow dim with waiting for my God. More in number than the hairs of my head are those who hate me without cause; mighty are those who would destroy me, those who attack me with lies. What I did not steal must I now restore? O God, you know my folly; the wrongs I have done are not hidden from you.

⋏ **Proverbs 23:20 ESV:** Be not among drunkards or among gluttonous eaters of meat.

⋏ **1 Corinthians 5:11 ESV:** But now I am writing to you not to associate with anyone who bears the name of brother if he is guilty of sexual immorality or greed, or is an idolater, reviler, drunkard, or swindler—not even to eat with such a one.

⋏ **Matthew 6:33 ESV:** But seek first the kingdom of God and His righteousness, and all these things will be added to you.

- **Proverbs 3:5-6 ESV**: Trust in the Lord with all your heart, and do not lean on your own understanding. In all your ways acknowledge Him, and He will make straight your paths.
- **Ephesians 5:18-20 ESV:** And do not get drunk with wine, for that is debauchery, but be filled with the Spirit, addressing one another in psalms and hymns and spiritual songs, singing and making melody to the Lord with your heart, giving thanks always and for everything to God the Father in the name of our Lord Jesus Christ.
- **Luke 21:34 ESV:** But watch yourselves lest your hearts be weighed down with dissipation and drunkenness and cares of this life, and that day come upon you suddenly like a trap.
- **Romans 12:1-2 ESV:** I appeal to you therefore, brothers, by the mercies of God, to present your bodies as a living sacrifice, holy and acceptable to God, which is your spiritual worship. Do not be conformed to this world, but be transformed by the renewal of your mind, that by testing you may discern what is the will of God, what is good and acceptable and perfect.
- **1 Corinthians 3:16-17 ESV:** Do you not know that you are God's temple and that God's Spirit dwells in you? If anyone destroys God's temple, God will destroy him. For God's temple is holy, and you are that temple.
- **Psalm 50:15:** And call upon me in the day of trouble; I will deliver you, and you shall glorify Me.**Bottom of Form**

"Bear with each other and forgive one another if any of you has a grievance against someone. Forgive as the Lord forgave you."

Colossians 3:13

CHAPTER 29
EMOTIONAL STAGES OF GRIEF AFTER FAMILY BETRAYAL

When family betrays you, a few things might happen in any order. For me, it was forgiveness first, then denial, then anger, bargaining, depression, acceptance, and hope. The emotional steps might be different for different people, but we all agree that the feelings after family betrayal are usually not good.

Forgiveness or Anger

The first thing when family betrays you is usually anger against that family member. However, if you make forgiveness or forgiving the first thing, you stand a better chance at a speedy recovery. I am not saying forgiveness is optional! I am simply reiterating that forgiveness means handing over that family member that has betrayed you to God. Always remember that forgiveness does not, in any way, shape or form, excuse their behavior. Forgiveness prevents their selfish behavior from destroying your heart. The last time I checked, the power to exonerate belongs to God and God alone.

What is forgiveness? Forgiveness is not a simple term as some of us may think. You know a word is powerful and spiritually entangled when even the notorious Oxford

Dictionary uses that same word to define the word. Forgiveness, as defined by the Oxford Dictionary, means "the action or process of forgiving or being forgiven". However, OD gives a series of similar words to help you understand the hidden spiritual meaning and wisdom behind this powerful word. Some of these similar words are: pardon, absolution, exoneration, remission, dispensation, indulgence, understanding, tolerance, purgation, clemency, mercy, pity, lenience, leniency, quarter, reprieve, discharge, amnesty, **DELIVERY**, acquittal, clearing, pardoning, condoning, condonation, vindication, exculpation, **LETTING OFF**, shrift, shriving.

From this list of similar words, you should understand by now that the power to forgive does not belong to you but to an authority higher than you, and heaven bound. Of all the similar words to forgiveness, you as a child of God can and should only deliver or let off your hurt and whoever hurt you to God as soon as it happens. The rest is up to God. Forgiveness to you as a child of God should be swift and sudden and purposeful. You don't have to understand anything before letting God handle your pain and perpetrator.

If this sounds confusing to you, I can relate and simplify it by giving you the opposite of the word forgiveness, according to the OD. If you don't forgive fast and on purpose, then you are either merciless or administering punishment. Keep this in mind: mercy belongs to God and whether you hand over your perpetrator to Him or not has nothing to do with His decision to show mercy on you or the person that has betrayed you. Always remember Matthew 7:1, "Do not Judge and you will not be judged. As you judge others, so you too will be judged". Pardon, exoneration, acquittal, discharge, leniency, vindication are all terms like forgiveness and used to describe actions taken after judging someone.

Bargaining

During the bargaining stage, you might question your character, and everything you thought about that family member. You question how your life will continue in relation to that family member and perhaps, in relation to your prior expectations.

Depletion or Depression

During this stage, you feel powerless, uncertain, vulnerable. Expecting that you can go to sleep one night and wake up the next morning already over the pain isn't realistic. Recovering from emotional wounds takes time. Family betrayal can cause a personal energy crisis. Searching for answers to why someone who is supposed to have your back is the very one stabbing you in the back can stretch you thin, stress you out, and completely drain you. Be careful not to confuse your depletion with depression.

Though you need to get enough sleep, water, nutrients, and exercise, a survey of endocrinologists, nutritionists, and sports medicine specialists by Boston-based psychotherapist Mira Kirshenbaum (in her book *The Emotional Energy Factor*) turned up an astonishing consensus: 70 percent of our total energy is emotional — the kind that manifests as hope, resilience, passion, fun, and enthusiasm.

Keep praying, singing, hoping and dreaming to build a solid energy that is stronger than any future betrayals and discouragements. Develop the daily skill of protecting and replenishing your emotional energy.

Kirshenbaum's approach is refreshingly down-to-earth. First, you plug the leaks. Learn to recognize what drains your energy—life situations, toxic people, or habits of mind like worry, guilt, indecision, and envy—and take steps to avoid or minimize them. Second, you identify what fills your tank—pleasure, prayer, novelty, anticipation, fun—and give yourself more. "Unlike physical energy, which runs down as we get older, emotional energy can increase the more you learn what works best for you," says Kirshenbaum.

Denial

During the denial stage, thoughts float on your mind. There is uncertainty! This can't be happening. Surely, it won't last. I cannot believe what just happened. Am I crazy? Is this all my fault? Am I that insufferable? Will I be okay? Did I enable them to betray me? Will the other family members betray me too? Am I the problem?

Acceptance

Accepting the reality of the fact that family that is supposed to be a haven is instead the place where you have found your deepest heartache is daunting but needed in order to move on. Reconciliation may eventually take place, but at present, accepting what's happened allows you to make the most of your life right now.

Hope

Family betrayals, broken bonds and unresolved differences can reap the timely fruits of redemption, forgiveness and healing in Jesus' name. Hope requires mindfulness, a hell of a backbone, and ultimately, a positive attitude of gratitude. Where there is life, there is hope and the Bible says, "Now faith is confidence in what we hope for and assurance about what we do not see" (Hebrew 11:1). "For in this hope we were saved. But hope that is seen is no hope at all. Who hopes for what they already have?" (Romans 8:24).

What the Bible says about God's promises

- **Deuteronomy 31:6:** Be strong and courageous. Do not be afraid or terrified because of them, for the LORD your God goes with you; he will never leave you nor forsake you.
- **Mark 13:12:** And brother will deliver brother over to death, and the father his child, and children will rise against parents and have them put to death.
- **Matthew 24:10**: And then many will fall away and betray one another and hate one another.
- **Matthew 10:21**: Brother will deliver brother over to death, and the father his child, and children will rise against parents and have them put to death.
- **Luke 21:16:** You will be delivered up even by parents and brothers and relatives and friends, and some of you they will put to death.

- **Luke 12:53**: They will be divided, father against son and son against father, mother against daughter and daughter against mother, mother-in-law against her daughter-in-law and daughter-in-law against mother-in-law.

- **Luke 12:51-53:** Do you think that I have come to give peace on earth? No, I tell you, but rather division. For from now on in one house there will be five divided, three against two and two against three. They will be divided, father against son and son against father, mother against daughter and daughter against mother, mother-in-law against her daughter-in-law and daughter-in-law against mother-in-law.

- **Matthew 10:35-36**: For I have come to set a man against his father, and a daughter against her mother, and a daughter-in-law against her mother-in-law. And a person's enemies will be those of his own household.

- **Psalm 9:9:** The Lord is a refuge for the oppressed, a stronghold in times of trouble.

- **2 Timothy 3:1-5**: But mark this: There will be terrible times in the last days. People will be lovers of themselves, lovers of money, boastful, proud, abusive, disobedient to their parents, ungrateful, unholy, without love, unforgiving, slanderous, without self-control, brutal, not lovers of the good, treacherous, rash, conceited, lovers of pleasure rather than lovers of God-having a form of godliness but denying its power. Have nothing to do with such people.

"Bear with each other and forgive one another if any of you has a grievance against someone. Forgive as the Lord forgave you."

Colossians 3:13

CHAPTER 30
JESUS' TAKE ON FORGIVENESS

When family betrays you through adultery or any other way, shape or form, always remember the story in the book of John about Jesus and the adulterous woman. In everything, give thanks to God by showcasing His love, mercy and the way to salvation.

> *"Jesus went unto the mount of Olives. And early in the morning, He came again into the temple, and all the people came unto him; and He sat down and taught them. And the scribes and Pharisees brought unto Him a woman taken in adultery; and when they had set her in the midst, they say unto Him, 'Master, this woman was taken in adultery, in the very act. Now Moses in the law commanded us, that such should be stoned: but what sayest thou?' This they said, tempting him, that they might have to accuse Him. But Jesus stooped down, and with His finger wrote on the ground, as though He heard them not. So, when they continued asking Him, He lifted himself, and said unto them, 'He that is without sin among you, let him first cast a stone at her.' And again, He stooped down, and wrote on the ground.*

> *And they which heard it, being convicted by their own conscience, went out one by one, beginning at the eldest, even unto the last: and Jesus was left alone, and the woman standing in the midst. When Jesus had lifted up Himself, and saw none but the woman, He said unto her, 'Woman, where are those thine accusers?*

Hath no man condemned thee?' She said, 'No man, Lord.' And Jesus said unto her, neither do I condemn thee: go, and sin no more." **John 8:1-11 (KJV)**

Lessons to learn from the story of the adulterous woman

- Avoid publicly announcing another's sin. The acknowledgment of sin is a divinely private affair.
- Repentance should never be forced upon anyone; it is up to the sinner to decide when and how to repent.
- God's laws supersede manmade laws. The law of Moses has been replaced by the higher laws of God.
- God never intended for man to be judge nor juror over sin and repentance.
- Repentance means continuous effort not to sin again.

God is able, this I know, for the Holy Bible tells me so!

- **Deuteronomy 31:6:** Be strong and courageous. Do not be afraid or terrified because of them, for the LORD your God goes with you; He will never leave you nor forsake you.
- **Ephesians 3:20:** Now to Him who can do immeasurably more than all we ask or imagine, according to His power that is at work within us.

- **Hebrews 7:25:** Therefore, He can save completely those who come to God through Him because He always lives to intercede for them.
- **Isaiah 41:10:** "So, do not fear, for I am with you; do not be dismayed, for I am your God. I will strengthen you and help you; I will uphold you with My righteous right hand.
- **Psalm 23:4-6**: Even though I walk through the darkest valley, I will fear no evil, for You are with me; Your rod and Your staff, they comfort me. You prepare a table before me in the presence of my enemies. You anoint my head with oil, my cup overflows. Surely, your goodness and love will follow me all the days of my life, and I will dwell in the house of the Lord forever.
- **Psalm 27:14:** Wait for the LORD; be strong and take heart and wait for the LORD.
- **Psalm 50:15:** Call on me in the day of trouble; I will deliver you, and you will honor Me.
- **Proverbs 3:5-6:** Trust in the LORD with all your heart and lean not on your own understanding; in all your ways, submit to Him, and He will make your paths straight.
- **Philippians 4:6**: Do not be anxious about anything, but in every situation, by prayer and petition, with thanksgiving, present your requests to God.

"Bear with each other and forgive one another if any of you has a grievance against someone. Forgive as the Lord forgave you."

Colossians 3:13

CHAPTER 31
IN EVERYTHING, GIVE THANKS TO GOD

When your spouse betrays you and rips your heart into a million little pieces, give thanks to God and march on. When your child betrays you and rips your heart into a million little pieces, give thanks to God and march on. When your sibling betrays you and rips your heart into a million little pieces, give thanks to God and march on. When your parent betrays you and rips your heart into a million little pieces, give thanks to God and march on. When your grandma, grandpa, aunt, uncle, cousin, nephew, niece and extended family betray you and rip your heart into a million little pieces, give thanks to God and march on.

In everything, give thanks to God. Sometimes, the emotional pain of family betrayal is far worse than that of physical pain. The first thing our flesh wants to do is to get revenge. If not physically, then in our minds. But be still and take your pain to God. Don't focus on your pain, focus on God. Go to a private place with no noise, then be still and relax in the Lord. You will receive the peace that He has promised you. When you cry out to Him in prayer, you will feel His comfort. He is in control.

Remember the times that He has helped you, other believers, and people in Scripture. God promises to help you and never leave you. Talk to Him, trust in Him, be still, and you will hear His calming voice. Rest upon His strength.

When family rips your heart into a million little pieces, you don't live inside of them to figure out what motivated their actions. For all you know, they may believe their actions were proper, so don't hate them. This doesn't justify their bad deeds. It is important to understand the difference between acceptable and unacceptable behavior, but acknowledging the possibility they were doing the best they could, can help you attain a less judgmental mindset. Besides, letting go of hate is good for you. You cannot hold joy in your heart if you hate someone.

The saying that "Friends may come and go, but family is forever" is not new to most of us. Growing up in Akum village in Cameroon Africa, this was very often stated, sang in songs, acted in plays, and implanted in the depths of our souls. If you had an upbringing like mine, you realize that even with your toxic family member, you are not in a position to walk away, or feel that you want to, or that it's even the right thing to do.

So, what do you do when a family member is literally ruining your life with their toxicity? What do you do if the mere thought of walking away from a toxic family member makes you feel like you are going against everything your ancestors on whose shoulders you stand tall have laid down for you? How do you deal with your feelings of obligation, confusion, betrayal and a broken heart? How easy is it to accept the fact that not everyone's family is healthy or built on the premise of mutual respect, love and support? How can you deal with the bitter truth that in your God-ordained family, some family members build you up and some break you down?

Betrayal by family is the ultimate roadblock. We can choose to act in ways that either favor or impede personal growth. We can become stuck in a bad moment forever or we can put it behind us for good. We decide our path by either erasing the imprints of betrayal by forgiving, throwing the act of betrayal away not the culprits, starting faith slowly but sure, regaining faith in oneself, detaching from untrustworthy people, and trying hard not to betray others. The wounds of betrayal can be ingrained deep in our subconscious mind, but by the grace of God almighty, they are possible to extract.

To make peace, always remember it is easier to find common ground when you take the higher moral ground. You must forgive those who betrayed you (including the unforgivable ones) as dictated by God's wisdom. How?

- By understanding that the ability to forgive is owned by God, not you. "A person's wisdom yields patience; it is to one's glory to overlook an offense" **(Proverbs 19:11).**
- When the wisdom of God dictates that you forgive your brother 77 times a day, it implies bringing your tormentor to God every time for God to deal with him. **(Matthew 18:22)**
- Justice is in the hands of God, not in man's hands! When you decide to play God, He gives you the stage.
- Don't let the bitterness in your spirit keep you in a prison of unforgiveness.

- Give your anger, pain and shame to God and let him heal your broken heart the best way he knows how.
- Remember Jesus died on the cross, so you don't have to nail yourself on one every day.
- The saddest thing about betrayal is that it never comes from your enemies, so embrace hope.
- God and God alone can restore your stolen years, dignity, happiness and give you beauty for ashes.
- Choose to forgive and watch God transform your mess into a message of hope for others.
- **Jeremiah 30:17**: But I will restore you to health and heal your wounds,' declares the LORD because you are called an outcast, Zion for whom no one cares.
- **Exodus 14:14:** The LORD will fight for you; you need only to be still.

On a practical note, don't allow family members who betrayed you the opportunity to hurt you any further. Stay away from them if you have to and do it for as long as it takes for them to change their behavior towards you, even if that is your mom, dad, brother, sister, grandparent, aunt, uncle, cousin, etc. Remember, people can change and that gives you some hope you can re-establish a connection with family members. But you cannot open your heart and home to them until they show true remorse followed by a permanent change in their actions. Even then, you must proceed with caution.

It is well! To God be all the glory! Amen!

God is able, this I know, for the Holy Bible tells me so!

- **Deuteronomy 31:6:** Be strong and courageous. Do not be afraid or terrified because of them, for the LORD your God goes with you; He will never leave you nor forsake you.
- **Ephesians 3:20:** Now to Him who can do immeasurably more than all we ask or imagine, according to His power that is at work within us,
- **Hebrews 7:25:** Therefore, He can save completely those who come to God through Him, because He always lives to intercede for them.
- **Isaiah 41:10:** So, do not fear, for I am with you; do not be dismayed, for I am your God. I will strengthen you and help you; I will uphold you with My righteous right hand.
- **Psalm 23:4-6**: "Even though I walk through the darkest valley, I will fear no evil, for You are with me; Your rod and Your staff, they comfort me. You prepare a table before me in the presence of my enemies. You anoint my head with oil, my cup overflows. Surely, your goodness and love will follow me all the days of my life, and I will dwell in the house of the Lord forever.
- **Psalm 27:14:** Wait for the LORD; be strong and take heart and wait for the LORD.
- **Psalm 50:15:** Call on me in the day of trouble; I will deliver you, and you will honor Me.

- **Proverbs 3:5-6:** Trust in the LORD with all your heart and lean not on your own understanding; in all your ways submit to Him, and He will make your paths straight.
- **Philippians 4:6**: Do not be anxious about anything, but in every situation, by prayer and petition, with thanksgiving, present your requests to God.

"Bear with each other and forgive one another if any of you has a grievance against someone. Forgive as the Lord forgave you."

Colossians 3:13

CONCLUSION
KNOWLEDGE, UNDERSTANDING AND WISDOM FOR THE FAMILY

Though your family may have ripped your heart into a million little pieces, continue to give thanks to God. Always remember that under heaven you can never be alone, for God is always with you. Call unto him in your day of distress, and he will rescue you. Hang in there and stay focused with an attitude of gratitude always. Your family members' most wicked intentions can never thwart the perfect plan of God for your life. Like Joseph, your family may have ripped your heart into a million little pieces to help facilitate the realization of your Godly ordained destiny. Forgive those family members that have hurt you but remember not to give them other opportunities to hurt you again. Family is not always forever; you may have to say goodbye to toxic family members to *save* your future. Always remember to give thanks to God, no matter the circumstances. It is well in Jesus' Name! Amen!

Some Knowledge, Understanding and Wisdom Tips for the Family

- The family environment or family culture is the most important component of the family unit.

- The family environment or family culture is more important than anyone who lives within that family environment.
- Have faith in the character of members of your family, not in their various titles.
- Understanding is the most important concept in the family. Knowledge of family without understanding of family is useless; wisdom of family members without understanding the family dynamics is utterly useless.
- Never speak in anger or grief when family betrays you and rips your heart into a million little pieces. Keep your mouth shut until your heart is back in the right place and your voice of reason returns.
- When family betrays you and rips your heart into a million little pieces, learn to accept the apology you never got because to forgive is divine.
- Though forgiveness does not excuse the behavior of family members who rip your heart into a million little pieces, it prevents their behavior from destroying the heart of the family member betrayed.
- When family becomes enemies and rip your heart into a million little pieces, cry out to God, "Deliver me from my enemies, O God; be my fortress against those who are attacking me" (Psalm 59:1).
- Just because someone is your family does not mean you have to keep them in your life if they are toxic. Sometimes, **blood** *means absolutely nothing!*

- Some family members are just not loyal to you. They are loyal to their need of you and once their need changes, so does their loyalty.
- When family become enemies and rip your heart into a million little pieces, go to God and remind Him of His promises, "Though I walk in the midst of trouble, you preserve my life. You stretch out your hand against the anger of my foes; with your right hand you save me" (Psalm 138:7).
- Forgive yourself for the blindness that let family betray you and rip your heart into a million little pieces. Sometimes, a good heart doesn't see the bad in a family member.
- When a family member shows you who they really are and not who you think or expect them to be, accept and treat them as such.
- Sometimes in life, the family member you will take a bullet for ends up being the one pulling the trigger against you.
- Hurting another family member who really loves you with lies, deceit and betrayal can end up being one of your worst decisions.
- When family becomes enemies and rip your heart into a million little pieces, go on your knees and remind God of His promises, "Even though I walk through the darkest valley, I will fear no evil, for you are with me; your rod and your staff, they comfort me" (Psalm 23:4).

- It is not your obligation to expose the family member who rips your heart into a million little pieces because doing so may delay or even deny an opportunity for forgiveness, redemption and healing. The family traitor will expose himself or herself for who they really are.

- When a family member betrays you and rips your heart into a million pieces, remember that "God is our refuge and strength, an ever-present help in trouble" (Psalm 46:1).

- When a family member betrays you and rips your heart into a million pieces, the betrayal reflects their character, not yours.

- The saddest thing about family betrayal is that it comes from the same people who are supposed to be on your side.

- When a family member betrays you and rips your heart into a million pieces, "May the LORD answer you when you are in distress; may the name of the God of Jacob protect you" (Psalm 20:1).

- Don't let other family members guilt you into being in contact with a family member who isn't good for your mental health.

- When family rips your heart into a million little pieces, remember that "The righteous person may have many troubles, but the LORD delivers him from them all" (Psalm 34:19).

- When a toxic family member betrays you and can no longer control you, they will try to control how other family members see you. The misinformation will feel unfair but stay above it. Eventually, other family members will see the truth just as you did.

▲ When family rips your heart into a million little pieces, cry your broken heart out to God, "Have mercy on me, my God, have mercy on me, for in You, I take refuge. I will take refuge in the shadow of Your wings until the disaster has passed" (Psalm 57:1).

▲ You can never control a family member's loyalty. Sometimes in a family, the people you love the most are the people you can trust the least.

▲ Remember that blood is what makes you related, but loyalty is what makes you family.

▲ When family rips your heart into a million little pieces, "Do not forsake wisdom, and she will protect you; love her, and she will watch over you" (Proverbs 4:6).

▲ There is no greater blessing than a family hand that lifts you, especially from a fall; but there is no greater curse than a family hand that strikes you, especially when you are down.

▲ When family rips your heart into a million little pieces, it's serious but it's not a military initiative. Please don't recruit other family members to join you and fight the family traitor.

▲ Sometimes in life, your delusion of what your family is, will be mercilessly shattered by the truth of what your family really is.

- When family betrays you and rips your heart into a million little pieces, give God the glory and change that family member's role in your life.
- When family betrays you and rips your heart into a million little pieces, "Discretion will protect you, and understanding will guard you" (Proverbs 2:11).
- Sometimes in the family environment, not every question deserves an answer. Some things are better left unanswered and, therefore, unknown. Sometimes, honesty does not bring peace and sanity. Protect your sanity.
- What you don't know may protect you from the deadly pain of knowing. Don't try to go after the family for explanations. Certain things in life cannot be explained. Protect your sanity!
- Some family members who stab you and rip your heart into a million little pieces will play victim and tell the world that they are the ones bleeding. Again, give God the glory.

"Bear with each other and forgive one another if any of you has a grievance against someone. Forgive as the Lord forgave you."
Colossians 3:13

SPECIAL ACKNOWLEDGMENT

With much excitement and gratitude, I hereby acknowledge an amazing lady, Brenda Hurd. We both met when we were 12 years old in the prestigious all-girls boarding secondary school (Our Lady of Lourdes) in Mankon Bamenda, near the west coast of Central Africa. Brenda's love for God and humanity was conspicuous in the way she talked, acted, and treated others.

Her intriguing story of love, family betrayal, forgiveness and redemption will blow your mind. She is a champion of hope for the hopeless and a voice to the voiceless. Her story is elaborated in her **BESTSELLER** entitled *Two-Time Bride: The Story of My Courtship, Marriage, Divorce and Remarriage to the Man of My Dreams.* If family betrayal has ripped your heart into a million little pieces, stay on your knees in prayers and grab a copy of Brenda's book. You can thank me later. In everything, give thanks to God.

Brenda's marriage became a divorce statistic when her relationship to her husband Gordon hit the rocks barely 10 years after they came to the altar to make their vows before God, family and friends. All she had left were memories of a fairytale wedding to the man of her dreams and questions which at the time seemed to have no answers. As the years passed by in her wilderness of despair, God reached out and touched both their hearts and, like Lazarus, their decayed marriage was brought back to life to stand today as a testimonial to couples everywhere.

As the Phoenix arises from its ashes, her marriage arose out of the grave after 6 years of divorce. Lazarus was in the grave only a few days, but their marital Lazarus was 6 years in the grave after going through all the motions, serving of divorce papers, decree Nissi, decree Absolute. Yet, it pleased the Lord to mend it all. They celebrated 21 years of marriage in grand style witnessed by over 250 guests and family. They continue to be a blessing and avail themselves as counsellors to many couples and church communities around the UK and abroad.

Two-Time Bride is a ride along in the lives of Brenda and Gordon as they share their experience of courtship, marriage, divorce, and remarriage to each other! This is an incredible but true story of love, forgiveness, and healing, in keeping with the key principles of their Christian beliefs.

Is your marriage burnt out and hitting the rocks? Do you wonder if there is hope for you? *Two-Time Bride* is testament to the fact that healing is possible, even for a dead marriage. May you find bliss in your marriage as you share this journey with Brenda and Gordon.

OTHER RESOURCES BY THE AUTHOR

My Letters of Gratitude to Jehovah God

Evangeline N. Asafor is originally from Cameroon near the west coast of Central Africa. As a little girl growing up, she had a dream of one day becoming an international agent of social change—a dream she thought her native country could not contain. So she migrated to the United States of America in October of 2000. One of her best days in America was the day she was sworn in as a US citizen! She made a promise to herself to be an asset to this great nation, not a liability. Evangeline has worked as a licensed practical nurse since 2004 in the areas of rehabilitation, hospice, and home health while attending school towards her greater passion of affecting social change as a criminal justice professional. One of Evangeline's worst moments in America happened when her husband was arrested for immigration irregularities, detained in Miami for eight months, and finally deported back to Cameroon. The nightmares—and God's unending presence that followed these events—prompted the writing of Letters of Gratitude. Evangeline holds a master of science degree in criminal justice and is currently pursuing a Ph.D. degree in criminal justice at Walden University.

My Sweet Mother's Doctrines of Gratitude and Her Final Rest with Jehovah God

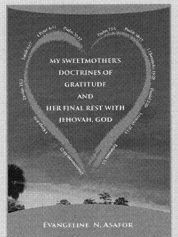

Today it's been over three years since my sweet mother, Mama Philomena Mbuh Asafor, was called to be with Jehovah God. Though I miss her so much and will never fill the vacuum her death created in my life, her doctrines and life of godliness, gratitude, unconditional love, loyalty, struggles, integrity, resilience, and steadfastness are my vital tools for success.

Though I cannot see or touch her, I know she is near. As I listen with my heart, I am able to hear her love all around me so soft and clear. I will continue to keep my sweet mother's memories in my heart until I meet her again, nevermore to part.

It is well!

God gives and God takes away. May Jehovah's name be glorified!

Gratitude as a Facilitator of Other Virtues in Jehovah God

Embrace gratitude as a worthy virtue, and the grace of Jehovah God will transform your life. Let it be your companion wherever you go, and you will reap life-sustaining benefits. Gratefulness-feeling or showing an appreciation of kindness; thankful Recognition-acknowledgment of something's existence, validity, or legality Appreciativeness-feeling or showing gratitude or pleasure Thankfulness-expressing gratitude Indebtedness-the feeling of owing gratitude for a service or forfeitability-able and grateful to learn God's love and insights by being taught Understanding-having insight or good judgment Devotedness-a state of being faithful Enthusiasm-intense and eager enjoyment, interest, or approval

Gratitude to My Ancestors on Whose Shoulders I Stand Tall

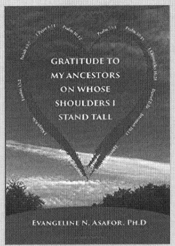

Thanks to the nourishment received from my rich cultural and spiritual roots supporting me, I humbly and proudly stand tall today. The wisdom that my ancestors shared generously has provided a shoulder and a platform on which I stand. I can never thank my ancestors enough for their crucial and meaningful contributions to my life as a village girl child raised on undisputed cultural and spiritual values. When I look back at my life growing up in a small African village and later moving into an all-girls boarding secondary school for five years under the guardianship of mostly Catholic nuns, an array of emotions come to me, from grateful tears, to sorrowful tears, and hearty laughter. The more I soul-search into the journey of ancestral wisdom that has brought me this far—from a small African village across the ocean to a town in America—the more grateful and empowered I feel in my God-ordained, purpose-driven life. It is important to celebrate my roots and my ancestors because they have nourished and defined the woman I am today.

AUTHOR'S BIO

Dr. Evangeline Asafor Ngwashi is a self-motivated, results-driven, and innovative professional with advanced knowledge in nonprofit management, leadership development, business management, and criminal justice. Dr. Ngwashi currently serves on the executive board of the proposed Hebrews Federal Credit Union as the Director of Compliance for the State of Florida. She is an Advisory Board Member for QualityMD, Funders USA, and College Food Network. From the healthcare perspective, Dr. Ngwashi has experience in Hospice Care, Geriatric Care, and Home Health Nursing. Dr. Ngwashi holds five degrees in Law and Business, including a Doctorate Degree in Criminal Justice and painstakingly conducted a novel research project on Financial Accountability in U.S Nonprofit Organizations. As an author, Dr. Ngwashi has published four books with an astounding global readership. As a motivational speaker, Dr. Ngwashi has provided tremendous value to the multitudes that have been opportuned to hear her.

To order additional copies of this book
or to check out our other quality custom-published books,
call 317-975-0806
or visit www.iempublishing.com
"Inspiring, equipping, and motivating — one author at a time."

Made in the USA
Middletown, DE
18 June 2020